So What's the Difference?

FRITZ RIDENOUR

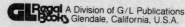 A Division of G/L Publications
Glendale, California, U.S.A.

Other good Regal reading:

Counterfeits at Your Door
by James Bjornstad
The Mormon Illusion
by Floyd McElveen
The Christian Life: Issues and Answers
by Gary Maeder with Don Williams
How to Decide What's Really Important
by Fritz Ridenour

The foreign language publishing of all Regal books is under the direction of *Gospel Literature International* (GLINT), a missionary assistance organization founded in 1961 by Dr. Henrietta C. Mears. Each year *Gospel Literature International* provides financial and technical help for the adaptation, translation and publishing of books and Bible study materials in more than 85 languages for millions of people worldwide.

For more information you are invited to write to *Gospel Literature International*, Glendale, California 91204.

Scripture quotations in this publication, unless otherwise indicated, are from the *New International Version* Holy Bible. Copyright © 1978 by New York International Bible Society. Used by permission.
Also quoted is *Phillips—The New Testament in Modern English*, Revised Edition, J.B. Phillips, Translator. © J.B. Phillips 1958, 1960, 1972. Used by permission of Macmillan Publishing Co., Inc.

Published by Regal Books Division, G/L Publications
Glendale, California 91209
Printed in U.S.A.

Library of Congress Catalog Card No. 67-31426
ISBN 0-8307-0721-2

The publishers do not necessarily endorse the entire contents
of all publications referred to in this book.

CONTENTS

When writing (or reading) about other faiths, you face the problem of going to one of two extremes: (1) criticizing and tearing down other faiths because you are secretly afraid that "maybe they're right after all"; (2) bogging down in syrupy condescension where you ignore crucial differences in an effort to "be fair."

So, at the start, the members of our editorial team (those who did the extensive research and writing on this book) set up four ground rules to help steer a middle course. These ground rules—which are equally useful to readers—include:

1. *A study of other faiths is not to be done in a spirit of criticism or ill will.*

2. *However, a study of other faiths is bound to bring up differences and disagreements.* To disagree with someone is not necessarily equal to criticizing him or tearing him down.

3. *See what you can learn from other faiths.*

This book is written from the orthodox Christian viewpoint. Its stated aim is to examine the real and basic differences between orthodox Christianity and some of the major religions and cults of the world. But while examining the differences, it is also possible to apply certain traits and characteristics in other faiths to the Christian life. Hindus and Buddhists, for example, have "far out" ideas on the nature of God, but they may have much to teach many Christians about why our daily rat race is keeping us from the peace of God that comes through completely trusting in Christ.

There are many other things a Christian can learn from other faiths, not to remake his theology but to help him examine himself to see just how deeply his own theology affects what he actually does and says and thinks.

And that brings up ground rule number 4:

To compare orthodox Christianity with other faiths in order to help Christians better understand their own beliefs.

The teachings of orthodox Christianity set it apart from all other faiths. Orthodox Christianity—the faith you find recorded in the pages of the New Testament—is unique because Christ is unique. His work was unique and the Scriptures that record that work are unique. We hope this book helps you see more clearly the answer to the question that most people have about other faiths: "So, what's the difference?"

Before preparing this revised edition we consulted with leaders in other faiths or scholars who are considered knowledgeable in a particular cult. We are grateful for the help they gave in correcting or updating the historical background and statements of belief in their particular fields of knowledge.

Fritz Ridenour

======= INTRODUCTION =======
So, What's the Difference Between What?

The "difference," as far as this book is concerned, is between the historic Christian faith and some of the major religions and cults of the world. Many books have been written about religions. Some have tried to show that all religions are basically the same, that they are just "different roads" that lead to the same God. But according to the orthodox Christian's Bible, all religions do not lead to God. There are differences—serious basic, and unavoidable differences—between the teachings of orthodox, biblical Christianity and the beliefs of, for example, Muslims or Hindus.

"Orthodox Christianity" means the beliefs held by the majority of Christians since the church began in the first century. These basic beliefs, as they are taught in the Bible, include:

- God became incarnate (flesh) in the man, Jesus.
- Christ atoned (paid for) man's sin through His death on the cross.

- Christ rose in bodily form from the grave, conquering death and proving He is God.
- The Bible is the inspired, authoritative, inerrant Word of God.

No religion, cult or sect in the world agrees with orthodox Christianity on all these points. The aim of this book, *So, What's the Difference?* is to explain exactly how other faiths differ from Christianity and what these differences actually mean.

It is hoped that this book will: (1) help the Christian better understand what other faiths believe and at the same time better understand what he professes to believe himself; (2) help the person who is "on the fence" spiritually speaking see just what the key issues are and (hopefully) decide to cast his eternal lot with Jesus Christ—not Christianity, not the church, not dogma, but Jesus Christ who is *the* Way, *the* Truth and *the* Life; (3) help the convinced follower of another point of view better understand Bible-believing Christianity and, at the same time, more clearly understand the faith on which he is staking his destiny in this life and eternity.

The biblical evidence for the orthodox Christian viewpoint is there. Chapter 1 reviews this evidence and it forms the foundation of this book. The major question is how you want to treat the evidence, which is summed up quite well in 1 Corinthians 15:3,4: "Christ died for our sins according to the Scriptures, that he was buried, that he was raised on the third day according to the Scriptures."

1
Orthodox Christianity
A Plumb Line for Comparing Faiths

"Orthodox" Christianity? What does that mean? Are there brands of Christianity that are "unorthodox"?

And "plumb line"? That's a tool used by masons to build walls straight and true. What does it mean to have a "plumb line" for comparing faiths? Some defining of terms is definitely in order.

The word "orthodox" comes from two Greek words that stand for "right belief" or "right opinion." As early as the second century, and even late in the first, Christians saw the need for separating right (true) Christian belief from various kinds of subtle heresies that began to creep in.

Today "heresy" or "heretic" is a loaded word. People tend to think of some wild-eyed reprobate skulking in the shadows. Actually many of the heretics that attacked the basic Christian beliefs were quite respectable and some even meant well. Webster defines "heresy" as "an opinion held in opposition to the commonly received doctrine and tending to promote division or dissension." Christianity has always had its foes, but no enemy has been more dangerous than the "enemy within"—those who hold opinions in opposition to the commonly received truths on which Christianity was founded.

From the Gnostics of the second century to the "God is dead" thinking of the present day, orthodox Christianity has faced challenges to the plain and simple teachings of the Bible: "Christ died for our sins according to the Scriptures, that he was buried, that he was raised on the third day according to the Scriptures" (1 Cor. 15:3,4).

As far as this book is concerned, orthodox Christianity is built on the ideas and doctrines contained in these two verses of Scripture. There are other important doctrines in Christianity, true, but in 1 Corinthians 15:3,4 is a "plumb line" for measuring the difference between Christianity and other faiths.

"Plumb line" was that other term that needed defining. In one of the shorter books of the Old Testament God says: "Look, I am setting a plumb line among my people" (Amos 7:8). A plumb line is a tool still used today by masons to make sure they lay up a brick wall straight and true.

Writing under the inspiration of God, Amos referred to this familiar tool to explain that God would measure men and their devotion to Him by His standards—by His Word—not man's.

In the same way God's Word will be the plumb line used in this book to define just what is "orthodox" and what is not. To find the difference between the basic truths on which Christianity was founded and what other faiths believe, this book will explore the teachings of the Bible on three key points.

These points—all contained in capsule form in 1 Corinthians 15:3,4—are: (1) the person and work of Christ (who He is and what He did for man); (2) the nature of man (a sinner in rebellion against God and in need of a Saviour); (3) the truth and reliability of the Bible (inspiration of Scripture).

Christ died. . .

By definition, the backbone of Christianity is Christ. The key questions concerning Christ are: His Person—who is He? His work—what did He do?

Of the great religions of the world, only Roman Catholics agree with orthodox Protestants concerning Christ's deity. All other religions (and most all cults) make Christ out to be only a man—a great teacher, a great example in His life and martyrdom—but still only a man. Following are some of the key questions that people often raise about Jesus Christ.

Was Jesus really God, or was He a great teacher and nothing more than that?

If Christ was "only a man" and nothing more, Christianity is a farce and not even worthy to be named with the world's great religions. The biblical record flatly, clearly and frequently states that Jesus Christ was God. For example, John 1:1 refers to Christ as the Word (Logos) and tells us that "in the beginning was the Word. . . and the Word was God." John 1:14 testifies that "the Word [God] became flesh and lived for a while among us."

Of primary importance is what Jesus said about Himself. On several occasions He claimed to be equal with God. See, for example, John 10:30: "I and the Father are one." On another occasion Jesus told Philip and some of the other disciples that because they had seen Him they had seen the Father as well (see John 14:9).

In Matthew 11:27, Christ claimed unique equality with God by saying that "no one knows the Son except the Father, and no one knows the Father except the Son and those to whom the Son chooses to reveal him."

In all the Gospel accounts Jesus claimed to be the Messiah. Jews who heard Him say this understood full well the weight of this claim. To them the Messiah was Christ, the Son of God. Jesus told the woman at the well that He was the Messiah (see John 4:25,26). While being "tried" by the

Jewish council on the night before His crucifixion, Jesus was asked directly, "Are you the Christ (Messiah)"? He answered, "I am." To the Jews this was blasphemy and they demanded that Jesus die. (See Mark 14:61-64.)

In summary, if Christ was not what He claimed to be (God), then He was a liar or a lunatic. As C.S. Lewis has said, He leaves us no other alternative.

Is Jesus' virgin birth a pagan myth?

Some faiths reject the doctrine of the virgin birth on the grounds that it is another legend, like pagan stories of heroes who were half god, half man. But in all pagan stories of this kind, there is cohabitation of a god with a human being. In the Scripture account, Mary is simply informed that "the Holy Spirit will come upon you, and the power of the Most High will overshadow you. So the holy one to be born will be called the Son of God " (Luke 1:35).

To deny the virgin birth is to repudiate the inspired Word of God, and make it impossible for Jesus to have been our Saviour. In order to have been a fully effective Saviour, Christ had to be God. Anything less would not have been sufficient. If Christ had been conceived through conception, with a human father, how could He have been eternal and preexistent? When an ordinary human being is conceived by human parents, a new "person" begins existence. But Scripture teaches that Christ existed from the beginning (see John 1:1).

Does the Trinity make "three gods"?

Some religions reject the Trinity on the grounds that it sounds like Christians worship three gods, not one. But perhaps an even stronger reason for their rejection is that the doctrine of the Trinity makes Christ coequal with God the Father. The Trinity is the particular target of critics in other religions and in many cults, particularly Judaism, Islamism, Unitarianism, Jehovah's Witnesses and Christian Science.

The orthodox Christian answer to the denial of the Trinity

is the evidence of Scripture. In the Old Testament it is true that Deuteronomy 6:4 states that "the Lord our God, the Lord is one." Yet, Genesis 1:26 uses the plural form, *elohim* for the word "God" as does Genesis 11:7. And in the divine appearance to Abraham in Genesis 18, the plural form of God is used again.

The New Testament also clearly states that God is one (see Gal. 3:20) yet here again you find abundant evidence that the unity of God, His oneness, involves three "persons." See for example Matthew 3:16; 28:19; 2 Corinthians 13:14. In addition, note that Jesus frequently referred to Himself as God (for example John 8:58), and John 14—16 teaches that the Holy Spirit enjoys the same interrelationship with the Father that Jesus does. The Son, Jesus Christ, is the God-man who was perfectly human and perfectly divine. He was one person having two distinct and separate natures. (See John 1:1,14; Gal. 4:4,5; Phil. 2:6,7.) The reason some people have difficulty with the Trinity is because they consciously or subconsciously try to reduce God to a mathematical unity that is familiar to human reason. They interpret the Creator in terms of the creature; that is, they see God as some kind of "big man."

How three persons can be only one (the Trinity) is a puzzle to natural reasoning. The question, however, is: "If God is supernatural—beyond nature—why must He be understood only in natural terms?"

The orthodox Christian accepts the mystery of God's greatness and the Trinity. *Baker's Dictionary of Theology* sums up the Christian's position: "The Christian learns to know God from God himself as he acted. . . and attested his action in the Holy Scripture. He is not surprised if an element of mystery remains which defies ultimate analysis or understanding, for he is only man and God is God. But in the divine work as recorded in the Bible, the one God is self-revealed as Father, Son and Holy Ghost, and therefore in true faith the

Christian must acknowledge the glory of the eternal Trinity.' ''[1]

Did Christ actually rise from the dead?

Orthodox Christians say He did and that the Resurrection proves Christ is God, that He conquered death and that He ensured all who believe in Him of eternal life. For Resurrection accounts, see Matthew 28:1-10; Mark 16:1-8; Luke 24:1-42; John 20 and 21.

The doctrine of the Resurrection is the foundation on which Christianity rests. As Paul wrote, "If Christ has not been raised, your faith is futile; you are still in your sins" (1 Cor. 15:17). Dr. Wilbur M. Smith, well-known American Bible scholar, comments in *Baker's Dictionary of Theology:* that the Resurrection doctrine teaches "the absolute uniqueness and the supernaturalness of the person of Jesus Christ, and the particular hope which he has brought to men. *No other world religion has framed a confession embracing such clauses as these.*" And in another place in the same article, Smith writes: "Remove the truth of resurrection from the New Testament and its whole doctrinal structure collapses, and hope vanishes."

Because Christ rose from the dead, the Christian has hope and assurance that he will rise also. The Christian's hope of resurrection is the subject of Paul's stirring passage in 1 Corinthians 15. And in 2 Corinthians 4:14 Paul writes: "We know that the one who raised the Lord Jesus from the dead will also raise us with Jesus."

If the Christian's hope is in a dead Christ who died as a martyr because He irritated the Jewish "establishment" then the Christian is in the same boat with the Muslim, the Buddhist and the follower of Confucius. Muhammed is dead. Buddha is dead. Confucius is dead. The Bible affirms that Christ is alive, and because He lives, the Christian will live also, eternally.

There are many other teachings concerning Christ: His

ascension (see Acts 1:10), His intercession in heaven for believers (see Heb. 7:25), His Second Coming. First Thessalonians 4:16,17 is one of the 300 statements in the New Testament on the Second Coming. But Scripture's teaching on Christ's person and work is stressed here in order to emphasize the first of three basic orthodox Christian teachings that will be compared to the views of other faiths discussed in this book. Christ died for a good reason. That reason is man's sin and God's love.

Christ died for our sins

People not only ask "Who is Christ?" They are equally puzzled over "Who is man?" Or, perhaps more to the point, "What is man?" Here are orthodox Christianity's answers to typical questions on who and what man is.

Is man all good, all bad or "in between"?

Most people wouldn't want to say man is "all good." There is too much evidence in the daily papers to the contrary. But neither do they want to admit that man is all bad. They prefer the "little bit of both" approach. Most of us, in fact, like to think we're "bad enough" to be fun (i.e., a regular type—not dull or "holier than thou"). But of course we're also "good enough" to "do the right thing when it counts." The typical eulogy said over many a man's grave is to the effect: "He was a great guy," when in fact he may have hated his mother-in-law, nursed a 20-year grudge against his neighbor, cheated on his income tax, padded his expense account, chased (and caught) several other women besides his wife, and blasphemed God daily in speech and actions.

Orthodox Christianity holds the unpopular opinion that man is "all bad." This sounds unreasonable until you examine what Scripture means by "sin." While it is true that on a social, human level, men display the capacity to do good, Scripture points out that all men are born with a "flaw in their nature"—and that flaw is original sin.

The Bible teaches that every man is born spiritually dead in sin (see Eph. 2:1) and that the reason for this spiritually dead condition is the sin of the first man, Adam. According to Genesis 1:26, Adam was made in the image of God. He was a free moral agent. Of his own choice, Adam sinned (disobeyed God) and the entire human race was plunged into sin. (See Gen. 3 for the account of the Fall.) Because Adam acted as "federal head of the human race" his initial act of sin had consequences for all men for all time. Paul wrote: "Just as sin entered the world through one man, and death through sin, and in this way death came to all men, because all sinned" (Rom. 5:12).

The nature of all men verifies that Paul is correct. All of us know by experience that we do not live up to all that we know we should do (or not do) in relationship to God and our fellowmen. The Bible knows it too and teaches that sin's roots are deep within man—in his heart, in his innermost being. "The heart," writes Jeremiah, "is deceitful above all things and beyond cure. Who can understand it?" (Jer. 17:9).

In the New Testament, Jesus, who "knew what was in a man" (John 2:25), did not bother to prove to men that they were sinners. He simply said that they were and that He had come to help them. Jesus' sharpest rebuke was for the self-righteous Pharisees, who did not think they were sinners. Note the irony in His statement in Matthew 9:13, "I have not come to call the righteous, but sinners." Jesus always cut through religious ceremony and sham to uncover the breeding place of sin—man's rebellious heart (see Matt. 15:1-20).

The Bible teaches, and modern anthropology affirms, that we are all of one human race. Scripture teaches that we are all descended from Adam, and because we are part of Adam's "family" (the entire human race), we all have Adam's nature—"a sinful heart." All mankind is under divine judgment due to sin. In his masterful development of universal condemnation of sinful man in Romans 1:18—

3:23, Paul shows that sin is not basically certain acts or deeds. Sin is the condition—the proud, rebellious attitude—of all men: Jew or Gentile, pagan idolater, moral middle-class citizen, or church-going religious man. And this brings up a standard question asked by everyone:

Just what is sin? Who decides what is a sin and what is not?

The answer is that God decides. There are many definitions for sin: breaking God's laws, going against God's will, etc. Summed up, these definitions might be stated: "Sin is proud, independent rebellion against God in active or passive form." Examples of active sins would be cheating, stealing or murder. "Passive" sin is more subtle. It includes not helping someone when it is within your knowledge and power to help him. It also includes the "uninvolved" attitude that says in effect: "Get lost, God, you are cramping my style. I'm too busy for you."

All of us sin actively and passively. As John puts it: "If we claim to be without sin, we deceive ourselves and the truth is not in us" (1 John 1:8). Isaiah zeros in on our basic nature this way: "We all, like sheep, have gone astray, each of us has turned to his own way; and the Lord has laid on him the iniquity of us all" (Isa. 53:6). The laying of our iniquity (our sin) on Christ is another puzzler for many people. They wonder,

How could Jesus Christ die for everyone's sins? Isn't every person responsible for his own sins?

Many religions and cults admit the problem of sin, but their solution is always different from Christianity's. While Christianity says that the only salvation from sin is faith in Jesus Christ and His atoning death on the cross, other religions seek salvation through good works or keeping rules and laws.

Orthodox Christians call Christ's death "the atonement." God's justice and God's love are involved here.

When Christ—God incarnate—died on the cross, He rendered satisfaction to God's holy standard and paid the penalty for the sins of all men. Equally important was that Christ's death demonstrated God's love and concern for all men, even those who hated God and wanted no part of Him. Romans 5:6-8 says it plainly: "You see, at just the right time, when we were still powerless, Christ died for the ungodly. Very rarely will anyone die for a righteous man, though for a good man someone might possibly dare to die. But God demonstrates his own love for us in this: While we were still sinners, Christ died for us."

In the Old Testament you can find an illustration of the "atonement" concept in the story of the Jewish Passover (see Exod. 12:1-14). The Israelites killed lambs without a blemish of any kind and smeared the blood over their doors. The angel of death that swept through Egypt that night taking the first-born in every home, "passed over" homes with this blood on the doorposts. In 1 Corinthians 5:7, Paul refers to the Exodus event when he says: "For Christ, our Passover lamb, has been sacrificed."

Paul is saying here that just as the Israelites were saved from physical death by the blood of a lamb when in bondage in Egypt, all Christians are saved from eternal spiritual death by the blood of the Lamb of God—Jesus Christ—who came to take away the sins of the world. (See also John 1:29.)

Scripture teaches that Jesus died "vicariously," that is, He was our substitute. For example, here is the teaching of the apostle Peter: "For Christ died for sins once for all, the righteous for the unrighteous, to bring you to God" (1 Pet. 3:18).

Scripture also teaches that Christ died *once*, for *all* men. His was a sacrifice that need not be repeated. "He has appeared once for all at the end of the ages to do away with sin by the sacrifice of himself" (Heb. 9:26).

Why does Scripture say that Christ's single death is

adequate payment for the sins of all mankind? It is adequate because *Christ is God*. No one less than God could make payment for the sins of all men. God is the One who set the holy standard. Who could fulfill its requirements but God Himself?

Scripture teaches that when a man places his faith and trust in the fact that Christ died to pay the penalty for his sins, he is ''justified.''

To be ''justified'' before God means that God's justice has been satisfied through the substitutionary death of His Son Jesus Christ. Christ paid the penalty for our sin, and He also removed the guilt for our sin. The removal of guilt is an important fact that many Christians overlook (or never really understand).

For example, suppose you have to go to court for speeding. But you do not wind up paying the fine. You learn that it has been paid by someone else—possibly good old dad or rich Uncle Charley. Getting your fine paid by someone else partially illustrates justification, but God goes one important step further. While the person with a traffic ticket might get his fine paid, it doesn't alter the fact that he is guilty. But when the sinner turns to God through Christ, his guilt is wiped out as well. As Paul puts it in Romans 5:1: ''Since we have been justified through faith, we have peace with God through our Lord Jesus Christ.'' (See also Gal. 3:6 and Phil. 3:9.)

In God's eyes, the Christian is completely pardoned for all past sins. We ''are justified freely by his grace through the redemption that came by Christ Jesus'' (Rom. 3:24). Not only that, God adopts us, makes us part of His family— spiritual sons and heirs. (See John 1:12; Rom. 8:16.) The Christian can't completely understand it, but he can say: ''God looks on me just-as-if-I'd-never-sinned.''

''Justified'' means pardoned by God for my crimes and also accepted by God, with a title to all the blessings that He bestows on His own. I am saved even from the guilt of sin, because God looks on me "just-as-if-I'd-never-sinned."

The Bible also teaches that man can do nothing to earn this justification. The Christian is saved by "grace"—God's unmerited favor, mercy and love. "For it is by grace you have been saved, through faith—and this not from yourselves, it is the gift of God—not by works, so that no one can boast" (Eph. 2:8,9).

The idea that "no one should be punished for my mistakes" is popular and widespread. It sounds noble, humble, and honest. Actually this thinking stems from pride, from not wanting to admit that no man can attain the standard of a holy God. "For all have sinned and fall short of the glory of God" (Rom. 3:23). "For there is no one who does not sin" (1 Kings 8:46). There is no perfect man. Therefore, no matter how carefully a man obeys rules or laws and no matter how many good works he does, he is still going to sin. He still falls short of God's perfect holiness. For a man to say that he can earn his own salvation is to say that God is something less than perfectly holy, and this is to say that God is less than God.

Christ died for our sins according to the Scriptures

Religions and cults the world over have their own view of what is meant by the word "Scripture." The Hindus have many sacred writings called the *Vedas*. The Buddhists have sacred writings called the *Tripitaka* (Three Baskets). Islam has its *Quran* (or *Koran*), dictated by Muhammed.

Cults often add to the Christian Bible in order to prove the particular points they want to make in opposition to orthodox Christianity. For example, the Mormons claim inspiration for the Bible, but also recognize other books (the *Book of Mormon, The Pearl of Great Price, Doctrine and Covenants)* as inspired. Christian Science says that the Bible is inspired, but also claims inspiration for Mary Baker Eddy's *Science and Health with Key to the Scriptures*.

Inspiration of the Bible is perhaps the main watershed

between Christianity and other faiths. If the Bible cannot be trusted to actually be the inspired Word of God, then its claims concerning the deity of Christ, man's sinful state, and man's need for salvation through faith in Christ's death and resurrection have no force. Following are orthodox Christian answers to common questions concerning the Bible.

Is the Bible actually "inspired by God"? Why is the Bible supposed to be superior to other books?

The *New International Version* translates 2 Timothy 3:16, "All Scripture is God-breathed." In other words, God, the Holy Spirit, operated on the minds of the authors of Scripture, revealing to them what He wanted written.

Dr. William Evans sums up the orthodox position on inspiration of Scripture by saying: "Holy men of God, qualified by the infusion of the breath of God, wrote in obedience to the divine command, and were kept from all error, whether they revealed truths previously unknown or recorded truth already familiar."[2] (See 2 Pet. 1:21.)

What kind of proof can Christians offer for the Bible's inspiration and accuracy?

There is, first of all, the Bible's own claim to be the Word of God. While this may not provide the kind of "proof" demanded by some skeptics, the biblical writers constantly affirm that they are recording God's words for man.

The Old Testament writers claimed divine inspiration through the use of the phrase, "Thus saith the Lord," or its equivalent, more than two thousand times. (For example, see 2 Sam. 23:1-3; Jer. 1:9; Hab. 2:2.)

Also note that the apostles themselves claimed they were inspired by God, that they spoke God's commands. Paul said that he wrote "the Lord's command" (1 Cor. 14:37). And Peter spoke of the "words spoken in the past by the holy prophets and the command given by our Lord and Savior through your apostles" (2 Pet. 3:2).

Apostolic authorship was one of the chief criteria in

deciding what books should be in the New Testament. The apostles were men who had served and lived with Christ. They actually had known Him or had experienced Him in a unique way as did Paul who was converted on the road to Damascus. The apostles suffered incredible persecution and died horrible deaths in the Christian cause. The only possible explanation for their zeal was that they had actually seen, talked with and eaten with the resurrected Lord Jesus Christ. If Christ had not really risen and had not appeared to the apostles, would they all have died for a lie?

The testimony of Jesus Christ Himself is vital evidence for the inspiration and authority of the Christian's Bible. Christians believe that Christ was God incarnate (in the flesh). The most important claim to inspiration for the Bible is what Christ Himself said about Scripture. Jesus constantly reaffirmed the inspiration of Scripture (the Old Testament at that time since the New Testament was not yet written).

According to Dr. Vernon Grounds, writing in *Christianity Today*,[3] Christ knew. . . believed. . . studied. . . expounded. . . venerated. . . respected. . . obeyed. . . and fulfilled the Scriptures. In short, says Grounds, Christ endorsed the Scriptures without qualification as the authoritative, errorless Word of God. Christ often criticized pharisaical interpretation of Scripture, but never Scripture itself. Christ based all that He said and did on Scripture. For some of Christ's own words concerning Scripture see Matthew 5:17,18; 22:29; John 5:39,40,46,47.

To claim something less than inspiration for Scripture is to claim that Jesus is mistaken or lying; and if He is either, He is something far less than God. And if He is less than God, His work of atonement on the cross for our sins is insufficient.

Another piece of evidence for the Bible's inspiration is its unity. The Bible was written by 40 authors over a period of 1600 years. Most of these writers never knew the others. When J.B. Phillips began work on his *New Testament in*

Modern English, he was not predisposed to regard the Bible as verbally inspired (that is, that the very words were inspired—God-breathed). But as the work progressed, Phillips was increasingly impressed and amazed at the unity that existed between the books of the Bible. He said: "In their different ways and from their different angles, these writers are all talking about the same thing and talking with a certainty as to bring a wonderful envy into a modern heart."[4]

The inspiration (God-breathing) of Scripture is the vital element that elevates the Bible above all literature. To say that Shakespeare's plays, for example, are as inspired as the Bible is to reduce Scripture to the level of human writing. Once you open this gate, the authority and power of the Christian faith is dealt a fatal blow. The Bible is God's revelation to man. You do not criticize revelation; you receive it. To put the Bible on trial before the bar of human reason is to make man too big and God too small.

Throughout history, attacks have been made on the Bible's accuracy and inspiration, but the Bible still stands. Men may criticize, disagree with, or reject the Scriptures, but they cannot conclusively prove that the Bible is not what it claims to be: the inspired Word of God to men. "Your word, O Lord, is eternal; it stands firm in the heavens" (Ps. 119:89).

Is orthodox Christianity "right"?

The Christian faith has many other doctrines besides the person and work of Christ, the nature of man and the inspiration of Scripture. In studying other faiths, however, you will see that these three key issues will continually come up.

The orthodox Christian believes that Christ is God and that He died for man's sins. The orthodox Christian believes that by nature, man is sinful, spiritually dead, and that his only hope of salvation from sin is faith in Christ's death and resurrection. And the orthodox Christian believes that he has a Bible that is inspired by the living God, the only infallible rule of faith and practice.

In order to have intelligent dialogue with other faiths, the Christian must know what his own faith teaches, what his own Bible says. Some point out that what the Bible says is not "final proof" that Christianity is right. The goal of this book is not to "prove that Christianity is right" but to clearly and fairly compare different religions and cults with the orthodox Christian faith. Orthodox Christianity is biblical Christianity. Orthodox Christianity is not watered down, rearranged or demythologized. Orthodox Christianity stands in faith and assurance upon the evidence "that was once for all entrusted to the saints" (Jude 3). And only God can prove something to a person, "No one who is speaking by the Spirit of God says, . . . 'Jesus is Lord,' [or be convinced that orthodox Christianity is right] except by the Holy Spirit" (1 Cor. 12:3).

Notes

1. *Baker's Dictionary of Theology* (Grand Rapids: Baker Book House, 1960). p. 448.
2. William Evans, *The Great Doctrines of the Bible* (Chicago: Moody Press, 1974), p. 195.
3. Vernon G. Grounds, "Building on the Bible," *Christianity Today* (November 25, 1966).
4. J.B. Phillips, *Letters to Young Churches* (New York: Macmillan Publishing Company, Inc., 1947). p. xii.

For Further Reading
Graham, Billy. *Peace with God*. New York: Pocket Books, 1953.
Lewis, C.S. *Mere Christianity*. New York: Macmillan Publishing Company, 1964.
Stott, John R. *Basic Christianity*. Downers Grove, IL: Inter-Varsity Press.

SECTION I

ROMAN CATHOLICISM

The only true church?

The only way to heaven?

Catholics and Protestants—
should they intermarry?

2
Roman Catholicism
The Only True Church?

Close to 600 million, more than one-sixth of the world's population, are counted as Roman Catholics. In the United States alone, the figure is more than 48 million. The influence of the Roman Catholic Church is incalculable.

Just what are the differences that divide Roman Catholics and Protestants? Many of these have to do with the office of "Pope." Catholics regard their Pope as the head of the Christian church, representative of Christ here on earth, and a direct successor of the apostle Peter. In other words, they regard the Catholic church as the "true church" of Jesus Christ.

Orthodox Protestants differ on all this and much more. But are these differences vital? How did all this controversy get started in the first place? Let's go back to the beginning.

How the Roman Catholic Church developed

Christianity began without fanfare, without uproar—with just the briefest word of command: "As the Father has sent me, I am sending you" (John 20:21). It sounds easy today. Nothing to it. But think about it for a minute. They were going out into a world that hated them. Jesus said, "I am sending you out like sheep among wolves" (Matt. 10:16). For many it would mean persecution, torture, death. Knowing this, why on earth did they go? No one bribed them to do it or forced them to do it. Then why? The answer is almost too simple to be believed.

They were sure that Jesus was exactly what He claimed to be. They were firmly and completely convinced that He was the Son of God, that He spoke to them with the authority of God. They loved Him and trusted Him. They wanted to do exactly what He said. It was just that simple.

A little later on, Jesus told them: "On this rock I will build my church" (Matt. 16:18). What rock did He mean? For that matter, what church? Was it Roman Catholic? Eastern Orthodox? Protestant (of one kind or another)? No, it was none of these. Well then, what church did He mean? What church did He establish? Which is the "true church" today? To find out, we'll have to trace the long history of the church through the ages.

The tiny spark that Jesus ignited in Jerusalem soon burst into a flame that leaped quickly along the shores of the Mediterranean—through Greece, Italy, Spain—through Egypt and Libya. Persecution only made the flame burn more brightly.

During the first 100 years Christians might well have been asking, "What is the true church?" Each local church exhibited variety in its structure and organization. Yet, even with their differences, their members were all called "Christians" and they all strived for the unity of self-giving love Christ displayed and Paul exhorted the church at Ephesus to attain. (See Eph. 4:3.) They were all believers, living, working, praying, dying together as they followed the teachings of their Lord.

Before the end of the second century the church at Rome held a distinctive place in the Christian world. Paul had said of the church at Rome, "I thank my God through Jesus Christ for all of you, because your faith is being reported all over the world" (Rom. 1:8). Rome was an important economic and political center, so by the fourth century the Christian church at Rome was very strong.

In an attempt to unite the church the Roman emperor Constantine, in the fourth century, declared Christianity the "official" religion of the empire. He gave church leaders— especially those in his capital city, Rome—enormous religious and political influence.

In the middle of the fifth century, Leo, bishop of Rome, commanded, through an edict from the emperor, that all should obey the Bishop of Rome because he held the "Primacy of St. Peter." Through the Pope, as Peter's successor, Peter would continue to minister as one who held the "keys to the Kingdom." Leo's claim was widely disputed, particularly by the eastern wing of the church (centered around Constantinople).

The break came in 1054 when the Patriarch of Constantinople (primate of the Eastern church) excommunicated Pope Leo IX of Rome. From that time on, the Western (Roman Catholic) church and the Eastern (Orthodox) church developed separately.

As the Western church grew, it began to add certain doctrines that were not in the Bible. Not everyone agreed with these new teachings primarily because they were not supported by Scripture.

Finally, in 1517, a leader of the opposition emerged. His name was Martin Luther. Luther did not intend to break with the church. He merely wanted to reform it, to root out the new teachings, to put fresh emphasis on the teachings of the Bible. Luther took the Bible as his one and only authority. He discovered there that the heart of the Christian faith is a direct and personal relationship with Jesus Christ. But the Roman Catholic Church rejected Luther's views, so he and other "protesters" were forced out. They began to meet separately. They studied the Bible, tried to interpret it for themselves, and followed its teachings as they understood them. This was the start of a new branch of Christianity called "Protestant."

And so, from a beginning with just *one* Christian church, today there are three main branches: Roman Catholic, Eastern Orthodox, and Protestant with its many denominations.

The ONLY "true" church???

Yet the Roman Catholic Church denies the validity of all claims but its own. It has stated, "We know that no other church but the Catholic Church is the true church of Christ. . ."[1] By what authority does the church make this statement? It is based on the Roman Catholic interpretation of the Bible.

Does this surprise you? Did you know that Roman Catholics accept the Bible as the inspired Word of God? It's true. Here's a recent statement on the subject: "Holy Mother Church, relying on the belief of the apostles, holds that the books of both the Old and New Testament in their entirety, with all their parts are sacred and canonical because, having been written under the inspiration of the Holy Spirit they have God as their author."[2]

But are Catholics allowed to read the Bible? Some people say they aren't, but that isn't quite accurate. The Catholic Church encourages Catholics to be nourished by the revealed truths of Scripture. However, to avoid disputes about essential truths, the Roman Church believes that the Holy Spirit ministers through the Pope.

"Scripture is subject finally to the judgment of the Church, which carries out the divine commission and ministry of guarding and interpreting the Word of God."[3]

Roman Catholicism teaches that "the Church is the divinely appointed Custodian and Interpreter of the Bible. . . God never intended the Bible to be the Christian's rule of faith, independently of the living authority of the church."[4]

Are the Roman Catholics right? Or does God want Christians to read His Word and interpret it for themselves?

What does the evidence show? Look at the language of the Bible. The New Testament, for instance, was written entirely in Greek—but not the classic Greek read only by poets and scholars. It was written in common Greek—the Greek that was spoken and read in homes and marketplaces. This proves nothing, but it strongly suggests that God wanted His Word to be read and interpreted not just by "authorities" but by common people as well.

What does the Bible itself say on the subject? In Deuteronomy 17:19, the man of God is told to "read it all the days of his life." The prophet Isaiah said, "Look in the scroll of the Lord and read" (Isa. 34:16). Jesus said, pointing out to the Sadducees, that it was dangerous not to know God's Word: "You are in error because you do not know the Scriptures or the power of God" (Matt. 22:29). The idea seems clear. Each one is to read and interpret for himself.

But someone might say: "All right, the Catholic Church claims to have sole authority to interpret God's Word, but don't Protestants take the same position? Don't they depend on their ministers to interpret the Bible? Aren't they equally wrong?" Well, it might seem so at first, but think a minute. Isn't there a significant difference?

Of course, the preacher (and teacher) has an important role. But did Christ ever say that the preacher (or teacher) is infallible, or that he has been given final authority to interpret God's Word? No. The New Testament picture is quite different. It is the individual studying God's Word, discovering the meaning, and then sharing this with others. For example, in Berea "they received the message with great eagerness and examined the Scriptures every day to see if what Paul said was true" (Acts 17:11). Paul wrote, "Let the word of Christ dwell in you richly as you teach and admonish one another with all wisdom" (Col. 3:16).

Protestants respect the preacher (and teacher) for his years of study, but they believe they are free to accept or reject his teaching. They believe that God speaks directly to each person from the pages of His Word and that the Holy Spirit helps each one understand the meaning of God's message. (See John 16:13.)

Now what has all this to do with the question, "What is the true church?" Simply this. The Roman Catholic Church bases its claim on its interpretation of events described in the sixteenth chapter of Matthew. But let's look at this chapter for ourselves. Let's see what we find without the benefit of any "official" interpretations.

"Upon this rock I will build my church"

In Matthew, chapter 16, we see Jesus with His disciples. They are in Caesarea Philippi, about 25 miles northeast of the Sea of Galilee. Time is growing short. Jesus knows that soon He will set out for Jerusalem—first, for a triumphal entry and, then, for death on the cross. Jesus has much to say. He wants His disciples to understand the meaning of what is about to happen.

Basic to everything was the matter of His own identity. Jesus brings up the question, "Who do people say the Son of Man is?" Why does Jesus ask such a question? Surely He knows what people are saying. His purpose is simply to get His disciples thinking about the matter.

That's why He asked, "Who do people say that I am?"

"Well, some say John the Baptist," they replied. "Some say Elijah, Jeremiah, or one of the other prophets."

Then Jesus asked them, "Who do *you* say I am?"

Simon Peter answered, "You are the Christ, the Son of

the living God." This was Peter's great confession of faith.

Peter had known Jesus for many months, perhaps more than two years. He had seen Jesus in all kinds of circumstances. Who Jesus was must have been a growing realization that suddenly came into clear focus.

Jesus' response shows the importance of Peter's confession. "Blessed are you, Simon son of Jonah," He answered, "for this was not revealed to you by man, but by my Father in heaven."

Now up to this point there's not much argument. The Scripture seems clear. But from here on, the going gets sticky. Think for a minute about what Jesus says next.

"And I tell you that you are Peter, and on this rock I will build my church, and the gates of Hades will not overcome it. I will give you the keys of the kingdom of heaven; whatever you bind on earth will be bound in heaven, and whatever you loose on earth will be loosed in heaven" (Matt. 16:18,19).

Now, how does the Roman Catholic Church interpret all this? Here is their view:

(1) The Christian church is built squarely on Peter; (2) Peter became first bishop of the local church at Rome; (3) Peter passed on "the keys of the kingdom" to his successors at Rome; and therefore (4) the Roman Catholic Church is the "true church" founded by Jesus Christ.

Roman Catholic teaching is expressed this way: "For our Lord made Simon Peter alone the Rock and key bearer of the church (cf. Matt. 16:18,19) and appointed him shepherd of the whole flock."[5]

Arguing that it is the true church, Roman Catholicism says, "For it is through Christ's Catholic Church alone, which is the universal help toward salvation, that the fullness of the means of salvation can be obtained."[6]

A look at the biblical evidence

But can we accept this interpretation? Certainly it raises

some problems. Look, for example, at some New Testament evidence about the early church.

Peter is never given a place of special authority in the New Testament. Jesus always treats the apostles as equal in authority and responsibility. (See Matt. 28:16-20.)

At the only church council mentioned in the New Testament, James—not Peter—presided (see Acts 15).

When the foundation of the church is mentioned, Christ—not Peter—is called the rock on which it is built. Peter himself explains in 1 Peter 2:4-8 that Christ is the cornerstone of the church. Paul also refers to "Christ Jesus himself as the chief cornerstone" (Eph. 2:20). "For no one can lay any foundation other than the one already laid, which is Jesus Christ" (1 Cor. 3:11).

The "true church" by biblical definition is built on Jesus Christ, and its members are those who confess Him as Saviour and Lord as Peter did when he said, "You are the Christ, the Son of the living God."

Some Protestant scholars (such as Luther and Calvin) taught that the "rock" of which Jesus spoke was Peter's confession. Peter had just said, "You are the Christ. . ." And Jesus responded, "On this rock I will build my church." What rock? This confession of faith. In other words, "all who confess me will be my church."

But suppose that the Roman Catholics are right. Suppose Jesus *did* refer to Peter as "the rock." Even if this is true, the text does not teach "apostolic succession." It does not teach that those who followed Peter were also to be the rock on which the church is built. Nor does the Scripture say anything about the authority of Rome or of popes. In fact, the word "pope" is not even used in the New Testament.

It all adds up to this: The Bible teaches that the "true church" is not some humanly-designed denomination or organization. The "true church" is simply the whole body of believers—those who through faith have a living relationship with Christ. (See, for example, 1 Cor. 12:27; Eph. 1:23; 4:12; Col. 2:19; John 10:9; 14:6.) In other words, anyone—whether he calls himself Roman Catholic, Eastern Orthodox or Protestant—can become a member of the "true church" of Jesus Christ. How does one become a member? That is the subject of the next chapter, and also another basic difference between Roman Catholicism and orthodox Christianity.

What's the difference?

Protestants	*Catholics*
	AUTHORITY
The Bible is their sole guide for faith and life (2 Tim. 3:16,17; 1 John 5:13; Deut. 12:32).	Both the sacred Scriptures and the sacred tradition of the church are to be regarded as authority for faith and life.
They are free to read the Bible and interpret its meaning—with guidance from the Holy Spirit (John 5:39; Rom. 15:4; John 14:26; 1 John 2:27).	Interpreting of Scripture is subject finally to the judgment of the church, "which carried out the divine commission and ministry of guarding and interpreting the Word of God."
No human being is infallible and only Christ is head of the church which is His Body (Eph. 1:22; Col. 1:18).	When the Pope speaks ex cathedra (from the chair) on matters of faith and morals, he, as Vicar of Christ—ruler of the visible church on earth, is infallible.

Notes

1. *A Catechism of Christian Doctrine*, no. 3, official revised ed. (Washington, DC: Confraternity of Christian Doctrine).

2. Walter M. Abbott, S.J., *The Documents of Vatican II* (Washington, DC: U.S. Catholic Conference, Publications Office).

3. Ibid., p. 121.

4. James Gibbons, *The Faith of Our Fathers* (New York: P.J. Kenedy and Sons), p. 63.

5. *Documents of Vatican II*, p. 43.

6. *Documents of Vatican II,* (Decree on Ecumenism 1,3). Quoted in *The Catholic Catechism* by John A. Hardon, S.J. (Garden City: Doubleday and Company, Inc., 1975), p. 242.

For Further Reading

Abbott, Walter M.S.J., ed. *Documents of Vatican II*. New York: Guild Books, 1966.

Boettner, Loraine. *Roman Catholicism*. Nutley, NJ: Presbyterian and Reformed Publishing Co., 1962.

3
Roman Catholicism
The Only Way to Heaven?

How can man be saved? Of all the questions that divide Protestant and Catholic, none creates a wider gulf than this. Where can we find the answer? We must begin with God's Word, the Bible. Why did God give the Bible? Principally to reveal His plan for man's salvation.

In the book of Romans, Paul takes the story of Abraham to illustrate God's plan. He asks, "What does the Scripture say?" And he answers, "Abraham's faith was credited to him as righteousness" (see Rom. 4:3). Abraham did good works, but these did not save him; he was saved by his faith in God. Paul goes on to show that all of us can be saved in just that way (see Rom. 4:23-25).

But to this simple plan of salvation (accepted by orthodox Protestants), the Catholic Church has added a series of complicated conditions.

The first key term is "sanctifying grace." What is it? Catholics say it is God's greatest gift. It was given to Adam and Eve who lost it when they sinned. Now man gains sanctifying grace only through baptism. Once he has received sanctifying grace he must follow a program of good works, or lose it.

This doctrine greatly concerned a humble but intelligent young monk named Martin Luther. Luther did everything that a monk of the early sixteenth century was supposed to do. He fasted, he whipped himself, he performed penances, he confessed even the slightest fault to a priest. Luther later wrote that no pen could describe his mental torture in struggling to achieve salvation through "good works." Because, despite his best efforts, he knew he still wasn't saved.

Luther's struggle did not escape the attention of his teachers at Wittenberg University. He was marked as a man of genuine dedication. One of the older professors commented, "This monk will confuse all the doctors. He will start a new religion and reform the whole Roman Church, for he bases his theology on the writings of the prophets and the Apostles. He stands on the words of Christ, which no philosophy or sophistry can upset or oppose."[1]

The prediction began to come true when, on the day that Luther pored through the Epistle to the Romans, a verse suddenly leaped out at him: "The righteous shall live by faith" (Rom. 1:17, *Phillips*). Luther found what he was looking for. The key to life is faith. Only faith is needed for salvation. The experience of having this verse come alive was Luther's "Damascus Road."

Orthodox Protestants believe that Luther's interpretation was right. Catholics, on the other hand, believe that his split with the church led to the breaking of unity—i.e., heresy. How exactly do Protestants and Catholics differ on the matter of salvation?

The Catholic definition of salvation

Protestants and Catholics agree that faith is basic to salvation, but Catholics say that a person must also do "good works'' to finish what was begun by faith, and that complete salvation comes through the church.

There are four terms we should know in order to understand the Catholic position on salvation. These are: Faith, Grace, Sin and Good Works.

Faith. What is faith for the Roman Catholic? Two things. It is faith in Christian truth as revealed in the Bible, and faith in the traditions and teachings of the Catholic Church. Catholics put the authority of the Scriptures and the authority of the "Church fathers" on equal footing.

As evidence, consider the Council of Trent (1545-1563). This was intended to settle questions that Luther and others had stirred up. At Trent, Catholic Church leaders stated that faith should be considered "the beginning of human salvation and the foundation and root of justification." But they also said, "If anyone shall say that man is absolved from his sins and justified. . . and that by faith alone absolution and justification are perfected: let him be anathema (cursed)." In other words, they held that mere faith in Jesus Christ is not enough for forgiveness of sins.

There is still another Catholic doctrine involving salvation that differs greatly from orthodox Protestant views. It is the doctrine that Mary, mother of Jesus, can pray to God for a person's sins. Belief in the power of Mary is so great in some parts of the world that some superstitious Catholics worship her in place of Christ.

Mariology (the study of Mary's role) contains statements like these: (1) Mary is the Mother of God; (2) her virginity continued after the birth of Jesus in that she never had any more children; (3) she was conceived without sin and lived a sinless life (the doctrine of the Immaculate Conception); (4) at the end of her earthly life she was taken up, body and soul, into heaven (the doctrine of the Assumption); (5) she is Co-Redemptrix; that is, she suffered with Christ and nearly died with Him and "may rightly be said to have redeemed the human race with Christ'';[2] and (6) she is Mediatrix or one who mediates between man and God. (These last two beliefs are not defined doctrines, but are held by many as such.)

Hundreds of shrines to Mary have been built all over the world. Fatima, Portugal, one of the largest, celebrated its sixtieth anniversary on May 13, 1977. Millions of pilgrims visit the spot where Mary is said to have appeared in 1917.

Another shrine to Mary is located in Washington, D.C. The Shrine of the Immaculate Conception is the largest Catholic church in the United States and the seventh largest in the world.

Many other saints of the Catholic church are revered by the Catholic believer. Catholicism teaches that these saints have attained perfection, so they can pray to God for those who are still striving.

Sin. Both Protestants and Catholics believe in *original sin*—that each of us inherited a sinful nature from Adam. But Protestants and Catholics disagree about how God forgives man. Protestants believe that faith in Christ removes sin, while Catholics believe that other things are necessary.

Protestants and Catholics also believe in *actual sin*. Actual sin is any willful thought, desire, word, action or omission that is rebellion against God. The Catholics divide actual sin into two categories: *mortal* and *venial*.

They believe that mortal sin is more serious because the one who thus sins must will to do it as an offense against God. Mortal sin causes a person to lose sanctifying grace and separates the human soul from God. Forgiveness for mortal sin can come only through confession to a priest or an act of repentance based on the love of God "for God's own sake."[3]

The more legalistic Catholics, like the Pharisees of Jesus' time, have made long lists of mortal sins. Here are some of them:[4]

- Missing Mass on Sunday or a Holy day without a good reason

- Getting seriously drunk
- Giving a bad example to your children in serious matters
- Stealing something expensive
- Reading non-Catholic Bibles or books about religion.

In addition to mortal sins, Catholics are concerned with venial sins. These are less serious. They do not take away sanctifying grace. They cause sickness of the soul rather than death of the soul. But venial sin is dangerous because it can lead to mortal sin. What are some of the venial sins?

- Lies which harm no one
- Gossip
- Getting slightly drunk
- Eating too much
- Stealing something cheap

Venial sins can be forgiven by a simple act of repentance.

Sacraments. Roman Catholicism teaches that faith is just the beginning of salvation, so the believer must constantly work throughout his life to complete the process. Here, the church is very specific. The believer must look to the seven sacraments of the church. *The First Communion Catechism* says: "A sacrament is a sign of Christ. It is Christ helping our souls. A sacrament . . . gives grace. What does grace do to the soul? Grace is life. It is God's life. It gives us power to please God."

The Seven Sacraments: steps in the "ladder to heaven"

A Practical Catholic Dictionary states that "God gave the Church these seven sacraments to take care of the spiritual needs in the lives of men." What are the seven sacraments and the Scriptures upon which they are based?

1. *Baptism* (Matt. 28:19). This is so important to Catholics that they hold that even a baby dying at birth must be baptized.

2. *Confirmation* (John 14:26). When a baptized child is 12 years old, he is confirmed. This ritual signifies that he is

strengthened in the faith. Catholics believe that this ritual gives him the Holy Spirit more completely.

3. *Holy Eucharist* (Matt. 26:26-28; Mark 14:22,23; Luke 22:19,20). The Holy Eucharist, or Holy Communion, is the most important sacrament of the Catholic Church. To the Catholic, communion is not just a symbol of Christ's sacrifice on the cross, but he believes that God changes the bread and wine into the actual body and blood of Christ.

Thus, to the Catholic, Jesus Christ is the actual sacrifice on the altar, the Victim whose blood and body are offered up several times daily in thousands of Catholic churches all over the world. They believe that the mass is an application of Hebrews 9:24-28.

4. *Reconciliation* (John 20:23). This is the sacrament by which sins committed after baptism are forgiven by Jesus through the ministry of the priest. To receive the Sacrament of Reconciliation worthily, a person must first examine his conscience; second, be sorry for his sins; third, have the firm purpose of not sinning again; fourth, confess his sins to the priest; and fifth, perform the penance (prayers or good works) the priest gives him.

Punishment in this life or in purgatory can be made lighter through indulgences. This is a power supposedly held by the church.

Indulgences can be gained in many different ways. Some examples of indulgences are: saying the Rosary (a series of prayers kept track of by counting beads on a string) or making the stations of the Cross (saying prayers at seven places around the church), or by visiting shrines—like Fatima in Portugal.

In the Middle Ages, indulgences were sold in the street. One indulgence salesman by the name of Tetzel infuriated Martin Luther. Luther wrote his famous *Ninety-Five Theses* in opposition to this and other practices. The selling of indulgences is no longer practiced by the

Catholic Church, but indulgences are still considered important.

5. *Anointing of the sick* (Jas. 5:15). Formerly *Extreme Unction*, this is the sacrament for the sick. "Extreme" means "last" and "unction" means "anointing with oil." Extreme Unction is thought to take away both venial and mortal sins even from an unconscious person who is on the point of death.

6. *Holy Orders* (1 Cor. 11:23,24). The Sacrament of Holy Orders places a spiritual mark on the soul of the person who receives it. It makes it possible for a priest to carry out sacred duties, such as baptism and communion, in the church. This mark can never be blotted out. This means that even though a priest might lead a sinful life, since he has received the Sacrament of Holy Orders, he can still function as a priest—that is, he can administer sacraments and forgive sins.

7. *Matrimony* (Matt. 19:6). Catholics also consider marriage a sacrament. The marriage contract is believed to be binding "till death do us part." The Catholic Church is opposed to divorce. However, some marriages are not valid if they are made without proper consent by people judged not capable of making such a decision.

These then are the seven sacraments that Catholics believe help them attain salvation. Now let's look at what the Bible says on the subject of salvation:

The biblical view of salvation

"As for you, you were dead in your transgressions and sins, in which you used to live when you followed the ways of this world and of the ruler of the kingdom of the air, the spirit who is now at work in those who are disobedient. All of us also lived among them at one time, gratifying the cravings of our sinful nature and following its desires and thoughts. Like the rest, we were by nature objects of wrath. But because of his great love for us, God, who is rich in mercy, made us alive with Christ even when we were dead in transgressions—it is by grace you have been saved. And God raised us up with Christ and seated us with him in the heavenly realms in Christ Jesus, in order that in the coming ages he might show the incomparable riches of his grace, expressed in his kindness to us in Christ Jesus. For it is by grace you have been saved, through faith—and this not from yourselves, it is the gift of God—not by works, so that no one can boast. For we are God's workmanship, created in Christ Jesus to do good works, which God prepared in advance for us to do'' (Eph. 2:1-10).

This is the clearest statement about salvation through faith in Jesus Christ found anywhere in the New Testament. Now, remember the Catholic and the Protestant views of salvation. Let's see how they agree or differ with the Bible.

Sin. Catholics and Protestants agree with Paul that all men are born in sin and are naturally separated from God. Paul wrote to the Ephesians that they were ''spiritually dead,'' and all men are still born that way.

Grace. There's a big difference here between Protestants and the Catholics. The Catholic, you remember, speaks of ''sanctifying'' grace as the only way man can get to heaven. But Paul, writing by inspiration of the Holy Spirit, does not say this. Nowhere in Scripture are there any qualifications on God's grace. Scripture says it is by grace and not by achievement ''that you *have been* saved,'' not ''*can* be saved.'' Paul continues by saying that this grace is not earned, ''It was nothing you could or did achieve—it was God's gift to you'' (Eph. 2:8,9, *Phillips*).

Moreover, this wonderful grace cannot be lost by the believer. Jesus taught that ''I shall lose none of all that [the Father] has given me, but raise them up at the last day'' (John 6:39). Jesus also taught that ''I give them eternal life, and they shall never perish; no one can snatch them out of my hand. My Father, who has given them to me, is greater than all; no one can snatch them out of my Father's hand'' (John 10:28,29). Peter adds that we ''are shielded by God's power until the coming of the salvation that is ready to be revealed in the last time'' (1 Pet. 1:5).

Faith. Grace is the unearned gift of God and faith is the channel by which this gift is received. Hebrews, chapter 11, talks about heroes of the faith. It points out how God worked through men who trusted Him.

Good Works. The Catholic believes that good works are necessary for salvation. But what does the Bible say? Are we saved by good works? No. ''It is the gift of God—not by works, so that no one can boast'' (Eph. 2:8,9). The Bible also teaches that good works are a product of our salvation—they come *after* salvation, not before. ''For we are God's workmanship, created in Christ Jesus to do good works, which God prepared in advance for us to do'' (Eph. 2:10).

So the heart of the controversy between Catholics and Protestants on salvation is that they disagree in their interpretation of key scriptural passages. Down through the ages, the Catholic has had to live under a burden similar to the burden of the Law that Paul wrote about in Romans 7 and 8.

As Martin Luther wrestled with the problems of his soul, he turned to the writings of a man who had done a lot of wrestling himself, the apostle Paul. In Paul's inspired words Luther found the answer that he spent his life proclaiming —the answer that has transformed the lives of millions of men and women: ''The just shall live by faith'' in Jesus Christ alone.

What's the difference?

Protestants	Catholics

SALVATION

God gives eternal life when the believer has faith in Jesus

Salvation is secured by faith plus good works—as chan-

Christ as his Saviour (Rom. 3:24; 5:1; Eph. 2:8,9; Rom. 10:9,10).

neled through the Roman Catholic Church.

They can be assured of salvation through Christ's work and God's promises (John 3:16; Rom. 5:18; Acts. 2:21; John 5:24).

They can never know if they have accomplished enough to satisfy God and actually attain heaven. Catholics feel fortunate to have the assurance of purgatory where they can receive temporal punishment that purifies them for heaven.

Notes

1. Edith Simon, *The Reformation, Great Ages of Man* (New York: Silver Burdett, Co., 1966), p. 20.
2. Pope Benedict XV, 1918.
3. Stanley I. Stuber, *Primer on Roman Catholicism* (New York: Association Press, 1960).
4. Rev. William J. Coogan, *A Catechism for Adults*, Adult Catechetical Teaching Aids (Chicago: ACTA Foundation, 1958).

For Further Reading
O'Brien, John A. *The Faith of Millions*, Huntington, IN: Our Sunday Visitor, Inc., 1974.
Rosten, Leo. *Religions of America*. New York: Simon and Shuster, 1975.

===================== 4 =====================
Catholics and Protestants
Should They Intermarry?

Dating, courtship, being in love, marriage—these are some of the things that have always intrigued young men and women. And chances are, this is the way it will always be.

A young person attending public school meets many people from many different backgrounds. Often a young person must face the question, "Should I date someone of another faith—especially a Catholic?" This question is very important, but to come up with a black and white answer isn't always easy. Sometimes dating gets serious. It may lead to going steady, then engagement, and finally to marriage. Then the question becomes even more complicated. It then asks, "Would I marry a person of another faith—especially a Catholic?"

Can we get some help from the Bible on this important question? First of all the Bible puts marriage on a very high plane. In Ephesians 5:31-33, Paul compares the marriage of a Christian husband and wife to the marriage of Christ and His church. Paul seems to be saying that the love of married

Christians should be generous and sacrificial, much like the love Christ had when He gave Himself for the church. How close is the marriage bond? In the Bible, a husband and wife are described as being "one flesh."

So what's that have to do with marrying a Catholic? Well, first, did you know that to marry a Catholic you must sign a very special marriage agreement—and you must stick to it for life? That's a fact.

What the Catholic marriage agreement says

Let's take a close look at what's covered in the Catholic Marriage Agreement:[1]

The non-Catholic signs this statement:

"I am clearly aware of the obligation of a Catholic spouse to preserve and profess his or her faith and do all possible to baptize and educate the children of our marriage in the faith."

The Catholic signs:

"Affirming my faith in Jesus Christ, I intend with God's help to continue living the faith in the Catholic Church. I respect the conscience of my partner in marriage. I sincerely promise to do all I can to share my faith with our children by having them baptized and raised Catholics."

What do you think? Are these the kind of promises likely to produce a harmonious marriage?

When two people become one in marriage, there is much to be *given* and much to be *taken* so that two lives blend happily into one. Healthy giving and taking can only occur when there is a sharing of viewpoints. But in the Catholic Marriage Agreement the non-Catholic who is a Christian gives up the right to share religious convictions with his wife—and possibly his children.

Is merely signing an agreement likely to end spiritual conflict between two people? No. In fact, it makes that conflict even more obvious. "Do two walk together unless they have agreed to do so?" (Amos 3:3).

The Catholic Marriage Agreement reaches even beyond the lives of the husband and wife into the lives of the children yet to be born. The Catholic must say, "I sincerely promise to do all I can to share my faith with our children by having them baptized and raised Catholics."

Four vital questions for Protestants

In the light of all this, there are at least four vital questions to be answered by every Protestant before marrying a Catholic.

1. Am I willing to have my husband (or wife) and children under the authority of the Roman Catholic Church?

We have already discussed the meaning of Catholic *authority*. The authority for all of its rules and regulations comes from the belief that both the Bible and the traditions of the Church are equally inspired by God. Thus, what some church father said in the fifth century is Catholic law today.

By signing the Catholic Marriage Agreement the Protestant agrees to submit *everyone* in his family—other than himself—to this Roman Catholic teaching. He agrees to let the Catholic Church teach his children that the Bible is not the sole guide of faith.[2]

The Catholic Church rules that, "The task of authentically (truly) interpreting the word of God, whether written or handed on, has been entrusted exclusively to the living teaching office of the Church, whose authority is exercised in the name of Jesus Christ."[3]

2. Do I consider the Bible the final authority for my life? Would it really matter to me to accept another authority?

The orthodox, Bible-believing Christian regards the Bible as God's Word, the supreme authority, the all-sufficient guide for life. He bases this faith on 2 Timothy 3:16,17: "All Scripture is God-breathed and is useful for teaching, rebuking, correcting and training in righteousness, so that the man of God may be thoroughly equipped for every good work."

3. Am I willing to have my husband (or wife and children) depend on the Roman Catholic way of salvation?

Here the Protestant and Catholic marriage partners are up against a real conflict. The Protestant may want to hold to his belief that salvation comes through Christ alone. But the rest of the family will believe that it comes through the complicated rituals of the Catholic Church. How could such a conflict ever be settled happily?

4. Am I willing to instruct and help my children and cooperate with my husband (or wife) as they work for their salvation within the requirements set up by the Roman Catholic Church?

Well, that's the agreement. The Protestant must agree to cooperate as the Catholic partner and their children work to gain salvation by attending Mass, going to confession and meeting the other requirements of the Church.

In a way, all four questions boil down to one basic question: Can a person who firmly believes in salvation through faith in Jesus Christ alone (see Rom. 3:24) have a happy and lasting marriage with a person who has made a solemn promise to put the demands of the Roman Catholic Church in place of a personal relationship to Jesus Christ?

Guidelines from the Bible

This matter of legalism versus faith is discussed in Philippians 3:1-11. Paul writes from personal experience. He tried to find salvation by obeying a man-made system. He tried to obey every detail of the Law as interpreted and embellished by the Pharisees.

When Paul first heard of Christianity, he recognized its threat to Jewish legalism and he persecuted it with great zeal (see v. 6). In doing this, he believed that he was completely right before the Law. Then, suddenly, on his way to Damascus to persecute some Christians, Paul's entire viewpoint was changed.

When Paul met Jesus on the Damascus Road he became a different person. Those things he had counted as gain—his legalism, his traditions—he suddenly saw as a loss, as meaningless next to the Person of Christ. It wasn't doctrine or tradition that had this transforming effect on Paul. It was the Person of Jesus Christ. It was not a theology, or a system, or a church. It was Jesus Christ Himself.

The result was that Paul came to count all things as loss compared to really knowing Christ. For Paul, "to live is Christ" (Phil. 1:21), not the following of rules and regulations.

There is no mention of a church or a system. There is no mention of the need for priests or sacraments. There is only continual and increasing emphasis on the need for a personal, direct relationship with Jesus Christ.

The Bible-believing Protestant who seriously dates or considers marrying a Catholic must think carefully. He must remember that, if he knows Christ as Saviour, his whole life is built on faith (see Rom. 1:17). Can he lightly give up a life of peace with God for a life of tension and frustration in marriage to a person with completely different views? Can such a marriage be happy? Does it even have a good chance of lasting?

Notes

1. This Catholic Marriage Agreement is the modified mixed marriage promise as a result of the Second Vatican Council.
2. Walter M. Abbot, S.J., *The Documents of Vatican II* (New York: Guild Books, 1966), pp. 117,118.
3. Ibid.

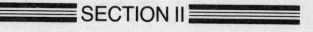 SECTION II

MAJOR RELIGIONS
OF THE WORLD

JUDAISM   "Hear, O Israel, the Lord our God, the Lord is one"—The Shema

ISLAMISM   "Muhammed is . . . the messenger of Allah and the seal of the Prophets"—The Koran, Surah 33:40

HINDUISM   "Many faiths are but different paths leading to the one reality, God"—Ramakrishna

BUDDHISM   "One's own self is most difficult to subdue"—Buddha

===================== 5 =====================

Judaism
Foundation of Christianity,
but Still Looking for Christ

What is a Jew? Is Jewishness a nationality, a religion, or both? What can we say to our Jewish friends about Jesus Christ, born a Jew, but rejected by His own people? (See John 1:11.)

These are some of the questions often asked about the people who follow one of the world's oldest living religions.

To begin with, the Jews were called "Hebrews." This name comes from "Eber," their traditional ancestor (mentioned in Gen. 10:21). We can go back even further to the name "Shem," a son of Noah (mentioned in the same verse). From Shem comes the word "Semitic" which refers to a group of peoples that includes the Jews and Arabs.

A short history of the Jews

But to the Jew (as well as to the Arab), his most important ancestor is Abraham. Abraham was descended from Shem (see Gen. 11:10-28). Abraham was a Hebrew (Gen. 14:13) who lived perhaps as early as 2000 B.C.[1]

The Bible describes a covenant or agreement between Abraham and God. God promised to make Abraham father of a great nation (see Gen. 12:2) that would someday inherit the land of Canaan (see Gen. 17:8).

Abraham's grandson, Israel (formerly known as Jacob), had 12 sons. These sons founded 12 tribes. Together the people were known as "the children of Israel" or "Israelites." After living as slaves in Egypt for hundreds of years, they were led to freedom by Moses. He brought them to the Promised Land, Canaan, later known as "Israel."

By the time David was king (1000 B.C.), Israel was a great nation, firmly established. David made plans to build a beautiful center of worship—the Temple—in his capital city, Jerusalem. Solomon, David's son, completed the Temple, one of the wonders of the ancient world.

On the death of King Solomon (about 922 B.C.) the nation of Israel was torn apart by a great civil war. It ended with the nation divided in two. The northern part was called "Israel," the southern was called "Judah."

Israel had a long series of corrupt kings who turned the people away from God. In 721 B.C., the Assyrians swept down on Israel and scattered the people.

Judah had a few godly kings, so it lasted longer. Finally though, the Babylonians conquered Judah and destroyed the Temple in 587 B.C.

When the Medes and Persians conquered the Babylonians, they freed the people from bondage. The people, now known as Jews, began to rebuild their Temple.

Judaism, the religion of the Jews, is built firmly on the Torah or Law. This Law had been given by God to Moses. At that time God promised that if the people would obey the Law they would be blessed.

After the Law came the prophets. These spokesmen for God stressed the importance of justice and love. They placed this far above keeping petty rules and regulations. Micah expressed it in these words, "What does the Lord require of you? To act justly and to love mercy and to walk humbly with your God" (Mic. 6:8).

This kind of decent behavior is still basic to Jewish thinking. For this reason, many charitable organizations are led and supported by Jewish people.

The Jews remained in their homeland until Jerusalem and the Temple were destroyed by the Romans in A.D. 70. Since then they have had no place to offer sacrifices for their sins. After this dreadful loss, they scattered to almost every nation in the world where they established communities and built synagogues to keep their faith alive.

The Jews have been persecuted many times, worst of all by the Nazis who murdered six million of them. In 1948, the Jews reestablished Israel. They have filled it with immigrants from more than a hundred different countries. In 1967, the Israelis captured Jerusalem, the first time they have held it as a free people since 586 B.C.

Jewish customs and laws

Judaism, the religion, today exists in three different forms: Orthodox, Conservative and Reform.

The Orthodox Jew tries to follow the letter of the Law. He studies carefully the *Torah* or Law written down by Moses. This Torah is actually the first five books of the Bible and, for the Orthodox Jew, it is the rule of life.

The Orthodox Jew not only obeys the Torah, he tries to observe certain other teachings that have been added through the centuries. Some of these teachings were written down around A.D. 200 in a book called the *Mishnah*. It is about a thousand pages long and consists mainly of instructions for daily living known as *Halakah*, or "the way to walk."

Around A.D. 500 another book of Jewish learning was compiled called the *Talmud*. The Talmud runs to about 36 volumes. It is based on the Mishnah, but much more material has been added, especially certain famous stories called the *Haggadah*.

These three books—the Torah, the Mishnah and the Talmud—rule every facet of the Orthodox Jew's life.

Take dietary laws, for example. The Torah—or Law of Moses—forbids pork or shellfish. Dishes used for meat may not be used for dairy foods. Animals must be slaughtered in a special way so that little blood stays in the flesh.

Orthodox Jews will not work, travel, use the phone, write, touch money or pose for pictures on the Sabbath. And there are many other restrictions.

Conservative Jews have a more lenient interpretation of the Torah. But they do believe that the Law is vitally important. Conservatives also want to keep alive the Hebrew language and the traditions of Judaism.

Reform Jews have gone quite some distance from Orthodoxy. They teach that the principles of Judaism are more important than the practices. Most Reform Jews do not observe the dietary laws or other laws, such as what a Jew should not do on the Sabbath.

But, whether Orthodox, Conservative, or Reform, all Jews agree on this: the Sabbath and the holy days must be observed. They have an old saying: "More than Israel kept the Sabbath, the Sabbath kept Israel."

For the Jew, the Sabbath begins at sundown on Friday night and continues until sundown on Saturday. In devout Jewish homes, as the sun is setting on Friday, the woman of the house, with her family around her, lights the traditional candles and gives the age-old blessing: "Blessed art Thou, O Lord our God, King of the Universe, Who has sanctified us by Thy laws and commanded us to kindle the Sabbath light." The father then blesses the wine, everyone has a sip, and then he slices the Sabbath loaf of bread.

After dinner on the Sabbath, Conservative and Reform families go to the synagogue. The main Orthodox service is on Saturday morning and they and most Conservatives attend another service in the afternoon.

The High Holy Days of Judaism are Rosh Hashanah (Jewish New Year, celebrated in September or October) and Yom Kippur, the Day of Atonement. These two days come around a 10-day period of repentance and soul-searching.

Another important time is the Passover. This usually comes about the time when Christians celebrate Easter. Passover in the Jewish home begins with a question from the youngest child, ''Why is this night different from all other nights?'' An older member answers, ''We were slaves to Pharaoh in Egypt. If God had not delivered our ancestors 'with a mighty hand and an outstretched arm,' we would still be slaves. That is why this night is different.''[2] Thus begins an ancient ritual and celebration that includes everything from prayers and special foods to games for the children.

Christians share a great deal with these Jewish people. To begin with, we share the Old Testament and its teachings. We share a belief in the same God—a God of holiness, justice, purity, righteousness and unity. Both faiths gladly proclaim, ''The Lord our God, the Lord is one. Love the Lord your God with all your heart and with all your soul and with all your strength'' (Deut. 6:4,5).

The moral and ethical teachings of the Bible are part of the Jewish and the Christian heritage. Both accept the Law as given by the living God who created the world and is still the Lord of creation.

There are many more similarities between Judaism and Christianity: the need to worship God, the importance of the family, the obligation to love others. Many Jews accept Jesus as a great prophet and find good things in His teachings. But this is as far as they will go.

Jesus Christ: the Great Divide
It is on the question of Jesus Christ—who was this

man?—that the Jew and the Christian divide. They began to divide even while Jesus walked the earth. You remember that the Jews of that time were looking for a Messiah (literally an "Anointed One") or Christ. He was spoken of by the Old Testament prophets as one who would redeem His people from their sins. But by the time of Jesus, tradition and petty legalistic interpretation of the Scripture had watered down belief in original sin and man's need for personal salvation. As a result, many Jews were looking for a national deliverer. They looked for a warrior-king like David who would drive out the hated Romans and restore the nation of Israel to its ancient glory. When we realize this, it's easy to see why many were disappointed by the humble Man of Galilee.

Yet Jesus claimed to be the Messiah, the Son of God. One day at a well in Samaria, He spoke to a woman. He explained how she might satisfy her spiritual thirst. Even this sinful woman knew that the Messiah was to come. Jesus replied that He was the one who had been promised. She believed and was saved (see John 4:7-26).

The New Testament contains many other references to Jesus as the Messiah or Christ (see Matt. 16:16; 26:63-65; Luke 24:26; John 8:28).

The Christian belief in Jesus as the Messiah is based on His fulfillment of Old Testament prophecies. He claimed to be the Messiah. The fact that He fulfilled prophecy proves His claim to be true.

• When King Herod wanted to find and kill the Messiah, he asked the Jewish priests and scribes where He was to be born. In Matthew 2:3-6 they remembered the prophecy of Micah (see Mic. 5:1-3) that He would be born in Bethlehem.

• The prophet Isaiah wrote that "the virgin will be with child and will give birth to a son, and will call him Immanuel. . . and the government will be upon his shoulders. And he will be called Wonderful Counselor, Mighty God, Everlasting Father, Prince of Peace" (Isa. 7:14; 9:6).

• Matthew quotes from Isaiah (see Matt. 1:23) to show that the Word of God was fulfilled in the birth of Jesus. In Jesus, God was with us. He is the Son of God, the Prince of Peace. All these titles refer to the One who came from heaven. He was sent by the Father to bring salvation to mankind! "He will save his people from their sins" (Matt. 1:21).

• Zechariah prophesied that the King would not come as a warlike conqueror, but rather humbly, riding on a donkey (see Zech. 9:9). On the day we now call Palm Sunday, Jesus rode into Jerusalem in just that way. Why? "This took place to fulfill what was spoken through the prophet" (Matt. 21:4).

The "suffering servant" of Isaiah 53

But perhaps the greatest of these prophetic passages is in the book of Isaiah. Beginning with chapter 49, Isaiah describes God's "servant," the Messiah King, who will suffer to redeem His people from sin.

Isaiah opens chapter 53 by predicting that the servant will be despised, rejected, sorrowful and full of grief (see v. 3). How perfectly this describes Jesus, who came to redeem the world, but was rejected, especially by His own people. (See John 1:1-12.)

Isaiah also describes the redemptive ministry of the Messiah. The Messiah would bear punishment for mankind's transgressions. (See Isaiah 53:4-6.) Peter (see 1 Pet. 2:24,25) reminds us that Christ died for all mankind and that His suffering brings us salvation.

Finally, Isaiah describes just how the Messiah will die. In the Gospels, we find Jesus fulfilling every detail of this prophecy. (Compare Isa. 53:7-9 with Luke 23:32,33 and Matt. 27:57-60.)

The Old Testament also prophesied His triumphant resurrection: "You will not abandon me to the grave, nor will you let your Holy One see decay" (Ps. 16:10). After Jesus' resurrection, Peter quoted this prophecy in the first Christian sermon (Acts 2:27-31). Many people had seen the risen Jesus. They knew that the prophecy had been fulfilled. They remembered what Jesus had said after His resurrection:

"This is what I told you while I was still with you: Everything must be fulfilled that is written about me in the Law of Moses, the Prophets and the Psalms. . . . This is what is written: The Christ will suffer and rise from the dead on the third day, and repentance and forgiveness of sins will be preached in his name to all nations, beginning at Jerusalem" (Luke 24:44,46,47).

So what's the difference between the Christian and the Jew?

The question of Jesus: Was He the Messiah as He claimed, or was He an impostor? Argument cannot settle this question. Each of us (whether Jew or Gentile) must look carefully at Jesus and answer the question for ourselves. Should we accept Him as Messiah, as the Saviour and Lord who was promised by the Old Testament prophets? As the Christ of prophecy, He stands ready to receive *all* who believe in Him. "For there is no difference between Jew and Gentile—the same Lord is Lord of all and richly blesses all who call on him" (Rom. 10:12).

What's the Difference?

Christians	*Orthodox Jews*
GOD	
One God is revealed in the Scripture as Father, Son and Holy Spirit—the Trinity. Within the one "essence" of the Godhead there are three persons who are co-equally and co-eternally God (Matt. 3:13-17; 28:19; 2 Cor. 13:14).	"Hear, O Israel, the Lord our God, the Lord is one" —The Shema

SIN

Man fell in Adam and is born in sin (Rom. 5:12; Ps. 51:5). All men are condemned before God for their sin: proud, independent rebellion against God in active or passive form (Rom. 1:18-23; 3:10,23).

Man is not born in original sin nor is he born good. Man is born free, with the capacity to choose between good and evil. Each man is accountable for himself.

SALVATION

Man is justified before God and obtains salvation through the atoning death of Christ on the cross. Salvation is a gift of God through faith (Rom. 3:24; 1 Cor. 15:3; Eph. 2:8,9).

Anyone, Jew or not, may gain salvation through commitment to the one God and moral living. Judaism looks to an afterlife, however, it does not stress preparing man for the next world as much as guiding his ethical and moral behavior in this present life.

JESUS CHRIST

Christ is the only begotten Son of God, the Messiah predicted in Isaiah 53. He is God as well as man. He was sinless and died to redeem all men from sin (Mark 10:45; John 1:13,14; 8:46; 10:30; Heb. 4:15; 1 Pet. 2:24).

While some Jews may accept Jesus as a good teacher of ethics, they do not accept Him as Messiah because (1) Jesus did not bring lasting peace; (2) Jesus was declared to be divine and the Jewish idea of Messiah is a man sent from God to deliver Israel from oppression, not to save individuals from personal sin.

Notes

1. John Bright, *A History of Israel* (Philadelphia: Westminster Press, 1959), p. 113.
2. Mordell Klein, comp., *Passover* (New York: Leon Amiel, Publishers, 1973).

For Further Reading

Ross, Floyd H. and Hills, Lynette. *Great Religions by Which Men Live*. New York: Fawcett World Library, 1975.
Vos, Howard F., ed. *Religions in a Changing World*. Chicago: Moody Press, 1959.

===== 6 =====
Islam
How Muhammed Used the Bible

Here's a good question for a TV quiz show: "What major world religion is the youngest, but so missionary minded that it makes almost as many converts in Africa as Christianity?"

The answer to that question is Islam, a religion that claims 700 million members and dominates 42 countries in Asia, Europe and Africa.

Islam is the correct name for the religion often incorrectly called Mohammedanism. The word "Islam" means "submission" (to Allah, the God of Muhammed who founded this religion). The members call themselves *Muslims,* meaning "those who submit."

How Muhammed became a prophet

Muhammed was born in Arabia in the city of Mecca in A.D. 570. He came from a prominent and highly respected family. When he was 25 he married a wealthy widow named Khadija. Their marriage was a happy one although only one of their children, Fatima, lived to maturity. Muhammed spent most of his time in solitary meditation. He began to have many disturbing visions. Once he believed he saw the angel Gabriel. Muhammed said that the angel gave him the following command:

> "Recite, in the name of the Lord who has created,
> Created man from clots of blood,
> Recite, seeing that the Lord is the most generous,
> Who has taught by the pen,
> Taught man what he did not know."[1]

The Arabic word for "recite" is *Quran* (often called *Koran*), meaning the reciting or the reading. Thus, the Quran, the sacred book of the Muslims, is the "reciting" of revelations given to Muhammed. Over a period of 22 years, Muhammed reported many other revelations. Encouraged by his wife, he began to preach in the streets and marketplaces of Mecca. Muhammed never claimed to be divine, but insisted that Allah had called him to be a prophet.

Muhammed hated the idolatry and the immorality of the Arabs who lived in Mecca or came there to trade their goods. He was met with bitter opposition, but for many years his influential uncle, Abu Talib, was able to protect him.

When both Khadija and Abu Talib died in A.D. 620, plots were hatched to kill Muhammed and his followers. Finally, on July 16, 622, Muhammed was forced to flee to Yathrib, a friendlier city to the north. This flight, called the *hegira*, marks the beginning of Islam. The Muslim calendar starts with this date, and the years are counted from "A.H." meaning "the year of the Hegira." Yathrib was later re-named Madinat an Nabi (City of the Prophet), in honor of Muhammed, but it's more commonly known as Medina. Muhammed became the religious and political leader of the city.

Soon the Meccans organized an army to destroy Muhammed and his followers. The fighting ended in 630 with Islam forces triumphant. Muhammed entered Mecca. He destroyed every idol in the Kaaba, the main temple, except the Black Stone, a sacred meteorite enshrined there.

Muhammed then declared the Kaaba to be the most holy shrine in Islam. Since that time it has been the spot toward which all devout Muslims direct their prayers.

During the next two years, Muhammed strengthened his position as the leading prophet and ruler of Arabia. He united the tribes into a vast army to conquer the world for Allah. His death in 632 did not lessen the fervor of his followers. They carried their faith across Asia, Africa, even into Europe—and to this day the growth of Islam has not ended.

The teachings of the Quran

The Quran is the sacred scripture of Islam. It is made up of 114 *surahs,* or chapters. These have been arranged according to length. The longest surahs are in front, the shorter ones are in back (with the exception of the first one). The ideas are all credited to God.

Muhammed's words were written down by his followers on everything from scraps of parchment to dried camel ribs. After he died, these fragments were collected and compiled into one book. Despite the fact that much of the Quran is scrambled and confused, Muslims claim it is copied from an original now in heaven.

As Islam spread across the world, various sayings and teachings were developed. These were finally written down in the *Hadith* (''tradition''). A saying in the Hadith is called a *sunna* or custom. This is thought to describe the way Muhammed thought or acted in a given situation.

The six doctrines of Islam

These are basic doctrines that every Muslim, from Morocco to the Philippines, is required to believe.

1. *God.* There is only one true God and His name is

Allah. Allah is all-seeing, all-knowing, and all-powerful.

2. *Angels*. The chief angel is Gabriel, who is said to have appeared to Muhammed. There is also a fallen angel named Shaitan (from the Hebrew, Satan), as well as the followers of Shaitan, the djinn (demons).

3. *Scripture*. Muslims believe in four God-inspired books: the Torah of Moses (what Christians call the *Pentateuch*), the Zabur (Psalms of David), the Injil (Gospel) of Jesus, and the Quran. But the Quran is Allah's final word to mankind, so it supersedes and overrules all previous writings.

4. *Muhammed*. The Quran lists 28 prophets of Allah. These include Adam, Noah, Abraham, Moses, David, Jonah, and Jesus. Of course, to the Muslim, the last and greatest prophet is Muhammed.

5. *The end times*. On the "last day," the dead will be resurrected. Allah will be the judge and each person will be sent to heaven or hell. Heaven is a place of sensual pleasure. Hell is for those who oppose Allah and his prophet, Muhammed.

6. *Predestination*. God has determined what He pleases and no one can change what He has decreed.

The five pillars of the faith

Besides the six doctrines to be believed, there are five duties to be performed.

1. *Statement of belief*. To become a Muslim, a person must publicly repeat the *Shahadah:* "There is no god but Allah and Muhammed is the prophet of Allah."

2. *Prayers*. This ritual must be performed five times a day. The Muslim must kneel and bow in the direction of the holy city, Mecca.

3. *Alms*. Muslim law today requires the believer to give one-fortieth of his income. This offering goes to widows, orphans, the sick and other unfortunates.

4. *Ramadan*. The ninth month of the Muslim lunar year

is called Ramadan. It is the highest of holy seasons. Muslims are required to fast for the entire month, but only during daylight hours. As soon as the sun sets, the feasting begins. During Ramadan, the believer must not commit any unworthy act. If he does, his fasting is meaningless.

5. *Pilgrimage to Mecca.* This is called the *Hajj* and must be performed at least once in a Muslim's lifetime. However, if the pilgrimage is too difficult or dangerous for the believer, he can send someone in his place.

How the Quran contradicts the Bible

The Bible has had an important influence on the teachings of Islam. For instance, the Arab proudly traces his ancestry to Ishmael, a son of Abraham. Muslim beliefs about the nature of God, the resurrection of the body, and judgment are very roughly similar to the teachings of the Bible. But there are some striking differences.

Following are some of the Muslim ideas that oppose what is taught in the Bible.

1. *The Quran denies that Jesus is the Son of God* although it describes the virgin birth in a passage similar to Luke 1:26-38 (Surah 3:45-47). The Quran calls Jesus a prophet, equal to Abrahan, Jonah and others, but places Him in rank far below Muhammed. Surah 4:171 says that "Jesus. . . was only a messenger of Allah. . . Far is it removed from His transcendent majesty that He should have a son."

Muhammed totally ignored the claims that Jesus made about Himself. Jesus said, for example: "I and the Father are one" (John 10:30); "Anyone who has seen me has seen the Father" (John 14:9); "Before Abraham was born, I am" (John 8:58).

The Bible also states that God Himself called Jesus His Son (see Matt. 17:5). Demons trembled as they recognized the Son of God (see Matt. 8:29). Doubting Thomas ac-

knowledged Him as "my Lord and my God" (John 20:28).
John identified Christ as the author of creation (John 1:1-5);
so did Paul (Col. 1:15-17) who also said, "In Christ all the
fullness of the Deity lives in bodily form" (Col. 2:9).

The only way to deal with this kind of evidence is to do
what Muhammed did—simply ignore or deny it. Muslims
claim that Christians have changed the Bible.

2. *The Quran says that Christ never really died on the
cross.*[2] "They slew him not nor crucified, but it appeared so
unto them" (Surah 4:157). How could this be? Well, according to Islam, Allah took Jesus to heaven just before the
crucifixion. But who died on the cross? It was Judas—made
up so cleverly to resemble Jesus that even Mary and the
disciples were fooled!

Of course, all this is in complete opposition to the teachings of the Bible. The Gospels tell us that Judas was the one
who betrayed Jesus (see Mark 14:10,11,43-45), and in re-
morse for what he did, he hanged himself (see Matt. 27:5).
Judas died at the end of a rope, not on the cross of Calvary.

As we have seen, the crucifixion of Christ was prophesied
in the Old Testament. Eyewitness accounts of that crucifixion
are contained in each of the four Gospels. The redeeming
death of Christ on the cross is the basic fact of the New
Testament. (See 1 Cor. 1:23; 2:2; 15:3,4; Gal. 2:20; 6:12,14;
Eph. 2:16.)

Jesus predicted His death many times (see Matt. 16:21).
Why did He die? As a "ransom for many" (Mark 10:45). He
promised that through His shed blood there would be "forgiveness of sins" (Matt. 26:28). The death of Jesus Christ,
according to Paul, was to end the animal sacrifices of the
Temple (see Heb. 9) because "Christ was sacrificed once to
take away the sins of many people" (v. 28). Jesus is the
"Lamb of God, who takes away the sin of the world" (John
1:29).

3. *Surah 4:111 declares that man must take care of his*

own sins. The Muslim must earn salvation from sin by following the "Five Pillars of the Faith." If he doesn't make it, it's his own fault for the Quran says, "Whoever goes astray, he himself bears the whole responsibility of wandering" (Surah 10:109).

But now, think of what the Bible teaches. Isaiah says that *all* have *sinned* (see Isa. 53:6). Paul emphasizes the same truth in Romans 3:23. Because of this, every book in the New Testament tells us that the only way man can find forgiveness is through faith in Jesus Christ.

Muhammed sincerely tried to lead his followers out of idolatry, but he proclaimed himself a prophet and designed a religion of rules and regulations. Like Judaism, the religion of Islam places on man a terrible burden of responsibility. But Jesus Christ has promised to lift such burdens from the human heart, "Come to me, all you who are weary and burdened, and I will give you rest. . . . For my yoke is easy and my burden is light" (Matt. 11:28,30).

What's the difference between Islam and Christianity? Simply this: Muhammed is only a dead prophet, but Christ is a living Saviour.

What's the Difference?

Christians	*Muslims*
GOD	
One God is revealed in Scripture as Father, Son and Holy Spirit. Within the one "essence" of the Godhead there are three persons who are co-equally and co-eternally God (Matt. 3:13-17; 28:19; 2 Cor. 13:14).	There is no God but Allah— *the* God.
JESUS CHRIST	
Jesus is the Christ, the Son of	Jesus Christ was only a man,

God, one with the Father, sinless redeemer of sinful man through His vicarious death on the cross and resurrection from the dead (John 1:13,14; Heb. 4:15; 1 Pet. 3:18; 1 Cor. 15:3).

a prophet equal to Adam, Noah, Abraham and Moses, all of whom are below Muhammed in importance. Christ did not die for man's sins; in fact Judas, not Jesus, died on the cross.

SIN

Sin is proud, independent rebellion against God in active or passive form (Rom. 1:18-23; 3:10,23).

Sin is failure to do Allah's will, failure to do one's religious duties as outlined in the "Five Pillars of the Faith."

SALVATION

Christ—God's Son—died for our sins (on the cross) according to the inspired Word of God (1 Cor. 15:3,4).

Man earns his own salvation, pays for his own sins.

Notes

1. Surah 9:1-5, the *Quran*.
2. The theories on Judas replacing Christ on the cross, Jesus' translation to heaven before the crucifixion, and Jesus' return to earth to comfort His mother and the apostles are found in most approved Muslim commentaries. See for example, George Sale, *The Koran, with Preliminary Discourse* (London: F. Warne and Co.), pp. 38,39.

For Further Reading

A.J. Arberry, *The Koran Interpreted*. New York: Macmillan Publishing Company, Inc., 1974.

Elder, J. *Biblical Approach to the Muslim*. Fort Washington, PA: Worldwide Evangelization Crusade, 1978.

Marsh, C.R. *Share Your Faith with a Muslim*. Chicago: Moody Press, 1975.

Miller, William M. *A Christian's Response to Islam*. Nutley, N.J.: Presbyterian and Reformed Publishing Company, 1976.

Hinduism
Every Man Is God

To the Western way of thinking, Hinduism is a strange way of looking at life. That's because we who live in the Western world (Europe and North and South America) have a heritage much different from that of the people of Asia.

Western thought began in ancient Greece where men like Socrates, Plato and Aristotle saw that the universe had a plan and purpose. To these early Greek ideas, Judaism and Christianity added the teachings of the Bible, which explained that this plan and purpose reflected the nature of a rational and energetic God who had created the universe. Because Western man believed this explanation, modern science was born. In other words, Western man became scientific because he was sure he could find law in nature. Why was he sure? Because he believed in a Law-giver.[1] The scientist today can look at a microbe, a plant or a star and see plan and purpose in their existence. He can also see exactly where they fit in the order of things. But remember, this scientific way of thinking got started because Western man believed in the God of the Bible.

Eastern man thinks on another wavelength

Things developed differently in the East. The typical Eastern man (the man of China, India, Southeast Asia) looks at the universe much differently. His religions teach him that all things that exist in the universe, including himself, are of no importance because they are temporary. He believes that the only important thing is the realm that exists out and beyond this world. He wants to reach this realm, and he thinks he can reach it only by completely denying the world around him. Can you see how difficult it is for any real science to come from attitudes like this? It's true of course that countries like Japan and China have recently been making scientific progress, but that's only because in the field of science they have adopted the Western way of looking at things.

Something else follows because of the completely opposite views that the man of the West and the man of the East hold about life; it is difficult for one to understand, or want to understand, the other. It is almost impossible for one to explain his views to the other.

However, let's see what we can discover and understand about the religions of the East, beginning with Hinduism. We will try to follow the mainstream of Hinduism and avoid the many branches that flow out of it. We will trace the growth of Hinduism from its beginnings in the Indus Valley to its arrival in Hollywood in the form of Vedanta—a modern version of Hinduism popular with many people from intellectuals to "hippies."

Origins and background of Hinduism

Hinduism came into importance about 2000 B.C. when the Aryans conquered the people of the Indus Valley. The Aryans brought their religion with them. It was a religion of hymns, prayers, and chants which, in time, were written down in what is now called Vedic literature. The *Vedas* are thought to be "revealed wisdom" and are as sacred to the Hindu as the Bible to the Christian.

Many gods populate the pages of the Vedas. These remind us of the gods and goddesses of Greek and Roman mythology. Like many other ancient people, the Aryans believed that these gods could cause death and disaster, so the object of their religion was to keep the gods happy.

Out of the Hindu system came a group called the *Brahmans* who performed the duties of priests. The Brahmans grew more and more powerful until they became the highest social class. They added more writings to the Vedas that they called the Brahmanas. These describe elaborate sacrificial rituals.

Around 500 B.C., still more writings were added to the Vedas. Their purpose was to establish a rigid class system. One hymn tells how four classes of people came from the head, arms, thighs and feet of the creator god, Brahma. The four classes are *Brahman,* or priest; *Kshatriya*, or warrior and nobleman; *Vaisya,* or peasant; and *Sudra,* or slave. The first three classes can take full advantage of all the Hindu religion has to offer, but the Sudras are not even allowed to hear the Vedas or to use them to try to find salvation.

Four stages and four goals in a Hindu's life

The Brahmans present an elaborate system through which salvation may come to members of the fortunate upper three classes. Each Hindu boy is first initiated. (Girls are not even worth mentioning according to this system!) He is then regarded as "twice-born." He then must go through the four stages of life: (1) a student; (2) the head of a house with wife and children; (3) a meditating hermit seeking enlightenment; (4) a homeless wanderer who has renounced all things of the world.

He is given four goals in life: (1) to become righteous and virtuous; (2) to have material goods; (3) to enjoy life through love, pleasure and appreciation of beauty; and (4) to have spiritual victory over life.

The writings of the *Upanishads,* composed between 800 and 300 B.C. added another way for man to attain salvation. These writings, also considered sacred by Hindus, contain a view of the world which is completely foreign to the Western mind.

The Upanishads teach that out and beyond this world is the *brahmanatman* (something like God) which is the only thing that really exists and has meaning. What man sees, the world of time and space, is *maya.* Maya is only temporary and has no real meaning. Yet everything that lives and breathes has an *atman,* or soul, which is part of the *paramatman* or world soul. Each individual atman, while existing in maya, is trying to get back to paramatman. All clear? Good, there's lots more.

Reincarnation leads eventually to moksha

The Upanishads state that the only way for the atman to get back where it belongs is through *samsara,* or reincarnation. A person's atman (soul) may begin as a worm, then through death and rebirth it goes high and higher in the order of things until it becomes a human being. Once the atman becomes a real human body, it must progress by attaining higher social classes. The human being attains a higher social class by following his *dharma*—his duty to do certain things according to the class he is in. These things include moral, social and religious duties—they are vitally important to the Hindu.

Another way to release the soul is through *yoga,* a discipline that holds one's physical passions in check so that the atman can escape the cycle of death and rebirth and be joined with the paramatman (world soul).

Once the atman has lost itself and its identity in paramatman, or the true reality, it is said to have passed into *moksha* (the infinite). Then and only then is the school of life over for the Hindu. He graduates into the infinite.

Hindus believe the world has no value

To sum up, the Hindu believes that this world is of no ultimate value because it is not permanent and that the only reality is something that he can get a glimpse of only through intense discipline and meditation. He believes that his soul has gone through a long cycle of birth, death, and rebirth and that it is doomed to continue the cycle until it finds release in moksha (the infinite). The Hindu believes that the Upanishads give him the wisdom he needs to reject this world in favor of the eternal paramatman toward which his soul is moving.

The teaching of the Upanishads still has a strong effect on the thought of Hindu religious teachers, especially those who came to this country with the Vedanta philosophy.

But despite long-lasting popularity, the Upanishad teachings have had critics among those of Hindu faith. The Brahmans, for example, taught that the soul could be released to "return to Brahman" only after reaching the Brahman class. This means, in effect, that the great masses of India who are poor and too illiterate to read the Upanishads are doomed to an endless cycle of samsara, death and rebirth. This view was challenged about 500 B.C. by Gautama Buddha who began to preach a "middle way" of salvation. Buddhism disappeared in India about A.D. 1000 when a new form of Hinduism arose.

This "popular Hinduism" quickly won favor with the people. New literature appeared, such as the long epic poems *Ramayana* and *Mahabharata*. There also appeared the *Bhagavad-Gita*, or the "song of the gods," which describes a way of salvation through worship of the god Krishna. There also appeared the *Puranas* which contain erotic stories about the gods and are very popular among Hindu villagers.

New Hinduism allows for as many as 330 million gods. Some 200 million people worship the god *Vishnu* and believe that he revealed himself to man at least 10 times. Vishnu has appeared as a giant turtle, as Gautama Buddha, and as Rama and Krishna, the two important heroes of the epic poems. Other millions worship *Shiva,* the god of fertility, whose rituals are as evil as those of the Canaanites whom God commanded the children of Israel to destroy.

"People's Hinduism" teaches that salvation can be attained by one of three ways: the way of works—that is, by following one's dharma, or duty; the way of knowledge as taught by the Upanishads; and the way of devotion to a god such as Vishnu or Shiva. The last way especially appeals to the lower classes (the vast majority of Indians) because it offers an easy way for their souls to make it to a higher class—and eventually moksha.

To the Western man. . . a hopeless hodgepodge

To the Western mind Hinduism sounds like a hopeless hodgepodge. It is filled with changes, additions and contradictions. Any attempt to put it into a logical system is like trying to repair a computer blindfolded while wearing gloves. But the people of India are comfortable with the complexities of Hinduism because it has grown with them since the beginning of their history. It is deeply embedded in their culture and they wouldn't dream of questioning it.

That's the biggest reason Christianity hasn't had much impact on the people of India. There are those, of course, who gladly accept Christ, but most reject the gospel because it seems to be too much a part of the alien Western culture.

A few forms of Hinduism have absorbed certain Christian ideas. Vedanta is a good example of this. According to Vedanta, the creator-god Brahman has incarnated himself in human form many times. He will do so again and again. Christ, Buddha, Krishna and many others are believed to have been incarnations of Brahman, which Hindus call avatars (super-saviours).

The followers of Vedanta believe that the most recent incarnation of Brahman is that of Sri Ramakrishna. Ramakrishna lived in Bengal toward the end of the nineteenth century. His followers say that he practiced all the spiritual disciplines of Hinduism, Christianity and Islam, and that he attained a vision of God in each one. Thus he was able to say: "Truth is one; sages call it by various names." Ramakrishna would often say, "Many faiths are but different paths leading to the one reality, God."

Vedanta, then, is friendly with all religions. Aldous Huxley, author of *Brave New World* and one of Vedanta's ardent followers, said, "It is perfectly possible for people to remain good Christians, Hindus, Buddhists, or Muslims and yet to be united in full agreement on the basic doctrines of the Perennial Philosophy."

But what does Vedanta have to say about Jesus Christ? Swami Prabhavananda says that a Hindu "would find it easy to accept Christ as a divine incarnation and to worship him unreservedly, exactly as he worships Krishna or another avatar (teacher) of his choice. But he cannot accept Christ as the *only* Son of God."[2]

What Gandhi thought of Jesus Christ

A similar statement was made by the great Indian leader Mohandas K. Gandhi: "It was more than I could believe that Jesus was the only incarnate son of God. And that only he who believed in him would have everlasting life. If God could have sons, all of us were his sons. If Jesus was like God. . . then all men were like God and could be God himself!" Gandhi said that he could not believe that there was any "mysterious or miraculous virtue" in Christ's death on the cross.[3]

Gandhi, like other Hindus, could not accept the Christian

answer to the problem of sin. And yet he felt a deep hunger for real salvation from sin. He wrote, "For it is an unbroken torture to me that I am still so far from Him, who, as I fully know, governs every breath of my life, and whose offspring I am. I know that it is the evil passions within that keep me so far from Him and yet I cannot get away from them."

How wonderful it would have been if Gandhi could have said with the apostle Paul, "What a wretched man I am! Who will rescue me from this body of death? Thanks be to God—through Jesus Christ our Lord!. . . Therefore, there is now no condemnation for those who are in Christ Jesus" (Rom. 7:24,25; 8:1).

Jesus Christ: the critical issue

Jesus Christ is the critical issue on which Hinduism and Christianity part company. The Hindu believes that God became incarnate (that is, took on human form) time and time again throughout history. The Bible teaches that God became incarnate only once in human history. And He came not just to teach man but "to take away the sins of many" (Heb. 9:28). When He comes again, He will come as the mighty judge of the living and the dead (see Rev. 20:11-15).

Christ gave proof of His claims. In John 5, He cited the witness of John the Baptist (v. 33); His own works (v. 36); the Father (v. 37); and the Scriptures (v. 39).

The resurrection of Christ is another great stumbling block to the Hindu. This refutes the Hindu teaching of continuous reincarnation and the Hindu belief that Christ is just another teacher-avatar (super-saviour).

The creed of Vedanta states: "We reject none, neither atheist, monist, polytheist, agnostic or theist. The only condition of being a disciple is modeling a character at once the broadest and the most intense. We do not insist upon particular codes of morality. . . Each is welcome to his own peculiarity, but he has no right to criticize the conduct of others."

By contrast, the Bible tells us that God came in Christ. Why did He enter human history? He came to die for the salvation of man. The Bible teaches that He rose again. But, to the Hindu, Christ is only one of many great teachers and there is no such thing as sin to be saved from.

Why the Hindu's god is too small

Actually, Hinduism is more a philosophy than a theology (a knowledge of God). The Hindus try to make a tremendous case for the "bigness" of their impersonal god—Brahman, the "that" behind and beyond reality. And where does the Hindu seek Brahman? In himself. For the Hindu, man is god. The Hindu's god is too small. The biblical record (see 1 John 5:11,12) states that God has given us eternal life and this life is in His Son. If we have the Son, we have eternal life (not a series of mythological, absolutely unproven reincarnations). If we do not have the Son, we have Gandhi's kind of assurance: ". . . an unbroken torture. . . that I am still so far from Him. . ."

The Christian, however, can say with Paul, "See to it that no one takes you captive through hollow and deceptive philosophy, which depends on human tradition and the basic principles of this world rather than on Christ. For in Christ all the fullness of the Deity lives in bodily form, and you have been given fullness in Christ, who is the head over every power and authority" (Col. 2:8-10).

What's the difference?

Christians	Hindus
GOD	
Eternal, personal, spiritual Being in three persons, as Father, Son, Holy Spirit (Matt. 3:13-17; 28:19; 2 Cor. 13:14).	Brahman is formless, abstract, eternal being without attributes. Takes form in a trinity as well as millions of lesser gods.

JESUS CHRIST

Christ is the *only begotten Son* of God, the Father. He is God as well as man; sinless; and He died for our redemption (John 1:13,14; 10:30; 8:46; Heb. 4:15; Mark 10:45; 1 Pet. 2:24).

Christ is just one of many incarnations, or sons of God. Christ was not the Son of God. He was no more divine than any other man and He did not die for man's sins.

SIN

Sin is proud, independent rebellion that separates man from God. It is falling short of the standards God has established in His Word to men. Sin must be punished, and its consequence is death and eternal separation from God (Rom. 3:23; 6:23).

Good and evil are relative terms. Whatever helps is good; whatever hinders is vice. Man cannot help "stumbling" over these obstacles as he strives to know himself. If he cannot succeed in this life, he may try again in reincarnated form.

SALVATION

Man is justified through the sacrificial death and resurrection of Jesus Christ (Rom. 3:24; 1 Cor. 15:3).

Man is justified through devotion, meditation, good works and self-control.

Notes

1. Alfred North Whitehead, *Science and the Modern World* (New York: Free Press, 1967), chap. 1.
2. Swami Prabhavananda, *The Sermon on the Mount According to Vedanta* (Hollywood, CA: Vedanta Press, 1972).
3. *Mahatma Gandhi Autobiography* (Washington, DC: Public Affairs Press, 1948), p. 170.

For Further Reading

Prabhavananda, Swami. *The Sermon on the Mount According to Vedanta*. Hollywood, CA: Vedanta Press, 1972.
Vedanta in Southern California. Hollywood, CA: Vedanta Press, 1956.

8
Buddhism
You Yourself Must Make the Effort

Unlike the Hindu religion, Buddhism can point to an individual founder and can look back to a date for its beginnings. The man who formulated Buddhism was Siddhartha Gautama, who was born a Hindu about 560 B.C. at Lumbini in what is now Nepal, near the border of India.

Tradition says that when Gautama was born, a seer prophesied that he would become the greatest ruler in human history. The seer added that if Gautama were to see four things: sickness, old age, death, and a monk who had renounced the world, the boy would give up his earthly rule and discover a way of salvation for all mankind.

Gautama's father, wanting him to become a great earthly ruler, built a palace for his son. He gave orders that neither the sick, the old, a dead body nor a monk could be allowed near the palace. Gautama grew up in this way, protected from the world. He later married a beautiful girl, Yasodhara, who bore him a son.

But the gods had other plans for Gautama. One day as he

rode through the park that surrounded his palace, he saw a man covered with terrible sores, a man tottering with age, a corpse being carried to its grave, and a begging monk who appeared peaceful and happy.

That night, as Gautama reported later, he began to think about the look of peace on the face of the monk. He began to wonder if there was more to life than the luxuries of his palace. Late that night he took a last look at his sleeping wife and child, then left the palace forever.

Gautama, 29 years old, was determined to solve the riddle of life. He shaved his head, put on a yellow robe and wandered the countryside as a beggar monk. First he studied the Upanishads with the finest teachers, but he could find no satisfaction in these writings. Then he tried to find salvation through self-denial. He starved himself until he was a walking skeleton, but this brought him no happiness either.

Gautama becomes the "enlightened one"

Finally, he sat under a tree for 40 days and nights. He swore that he would not move until he found what he was searching for. During this time, Mara (the evil one) tried to make him give up his quest. Then, at the end of the 40 days he experienced *nirvana* (the final state). He felt that he had found salvation. From then on, he was known as "Buddha" or the "enlightened one."

After this experience, Gautama Buddha went back to the world of man. He began to preach and teach about the meaning of life and his way of salvation. Soon, he founded the *Sangha,* an order of monks. By the time Gautama Buddha died, 45 years later, many thousands had accepted his religion.

In some ways, Buddhism is similar to the Hinduism from which it evolved. But in other ways, it is quite different.

Buddha denied that the Vedas and the Upanishads were divine writings. He said they were of no help in finding the way of salvation. He also denied that man has an atman (soul) which is a part of the paramatman (world soul), and that the present world is maya (unreal). He did accept the Hindu teachings on reincarnation along with *karma* (the duty one has to perform according to his station in life).

The Middle Way and the Four Noble Truths

But most important was Buddha's theory of the "Middle Way." For Buddha, the Middle Way is a spiritual path of salvation that winds between the complicated religion of the Hindus and the world of sensuality that he had known.

Buddha strongly opposed the caste system of the Hindus. You remember that the Hindus teach that a person must reach the Brahman caste through reincarnation before he can attain moksha, the infinite. Buddha taught that nirvana (the infinite) is for anyone regardless of caste. This made Buddhism very appealing, especially to the lower classes.

Instead of the hard-to-define teachings of Hinduism, Buddhism offers clear, firm rules for its followers. When Buddha preached in Benares, India, he presented the four main principles of Buddhism. These have come to be called the "Four Noble Truths."

These are the Four Noble Truths:

1. *Suffering is universal*. By this the Buddhist means that the very act of living must include suffering. In each of a person's incarnations, he must suffer. Salvation (nirvana) is to be released from this unending cycle of suffering.

2. *The cause of suffering is craving (selfish desire)*. Man remains in this endless cycle because he is too attached to the world. The Buddhist calls this *tanha*, or desire.

3. *The cure for suffering is to eliminate craving*. Since to live is to suffer, and since suffering is caused by craving, if craving were removed, suffering would be over. This was Buddha's great discovery: if a person could put an end to craving, he would put an end to suffering.

4. *Eliminate craving by following the Middle Way—the Noble Eightfold Path.*

Thus Buddha did what the Hindus could not do. He isolated the cause of man's inability to escape from the squirrel cage of death and rebirth, and he gave it a name, tanha. Next he worked out a system by which man could rid himself of tanha. This system he called the "Eightfold Path."

The Eightfold Path consists of eight ways of right living: (1) right viewpoint, (2) right aspiration, (3) right speech, (4) right behavior, (5) right occupation, (6) right effort, (7) right mindfulness, and (8) right meditation.

Buddha claimed that whoever could follow this Eightfold Path would eventually reach nirvana, a release from the endless cycle of death and rebirth. When Buddha was asked to define the state of nirvana, he always said that he had never tried to solve this question. His mission was to show man the way to escape the suffering of life, not to describe what he would find once he had been liberated.

Hinduism says that life in this world is meaningless. Buddhism says that life in this world is quite real. It involves real suffering, but because of this suffering, the world must be escaped.

Buddhism has always had great appeal for the peoples of the East. Unlike the elitist ideas of Hinduism, Buddhism offers a precise definition of man's problem along with an exact "plan of salvation" for everyone.

Buddhism was popular in India for several centuries until it was driven out by "reformed" Hinduism and the new Muslim faith.

During the first thousand years after Christ, while the gospel was being carried all over Europe, Buddhist monks took their religion along the trade routes to China, Japan and Tibet. Today, from Ceylon to Japan, there are probably half a billion people who follow the teachings of Buddha.

Twentieth century forms of Buddhism

Twentieth-century Buddhism takes a wide variety of forms. In Tibet, it's demon worship; in Japan, it's the new militant, nationalistic cult of Soka Gokkai. But the two main forms of Buddhism are *Hinayana* and *Mahayana*.

Hinayana means "the doctrine of the lesser way," referring to the belief that only a fortunate few can find nirvana—those who absolutely follow the way of Buddha. Since this was a derogatory name given by critics, the name was later changed to Theravada Buddhism. Theravada (the way of the elders) emphasizes the monastic life. This branch of Buddhism has become very wealthy through gifts of land and money for monasteries. Theravada Buddhism is dominant today in Ceylon, Burma, Thailand, Cambodia, and Laos.

Mahayana, the teaching of the "greater way," teaches that Buddha believed that salvation is for all people. Buddha taught that only man could save himself, but Mahayana developed the idea of a saviour god. This was their reasoning: Buddha had remained on the earth for 45 years. He could have gone to nirvana. Instead, he decided to stay to save mankind. Thus Buddha (and others like him) was a saviour to mankind and can still be called on by the faithful.

From all this, you can see that Theravada and Mahayana differ radically in their opinion of Buddha. To Theravada, Buddha was only a teacher (as Buddha himself claimed), but Mahayana has raised him to the position of a saviour-god for all people. Because of this, Mahayana Buddhism is by far the more popular. It is influential in China, Tibet, Japan, Vietnam and Korea.

Buddhism still enjoys phenomenal growth, not only in Asia, but in the West, so we must ask the question, "How well does it answer the needs of mankind?"

Buddhism claims that wherever it has gone it has raised the ethics of people, promoting honesty, sexual morality, and sobriety. On the other hand, Buddhism criticizes the Christian West for wars and the use of nuclear bombs. Of course, this is about as ridiculous as for a Jew to assert that Christianity produced Nazism. Buddhists have also conveniently forgotten that much of the trouble in recent years in Southeast Asia has been caused by ambitious Buddhist monks.

Buddhism also claims that it is designed to do away with suffering. This would be more convincing if Buddhists were active in social work, but actually they have done almost nothing in this field. The Buddhist thinks that escape from suffering is one's own personal row to hoe. He wouldn't dream of interfering with someone else's problems. The Buddhist has a fatalistic view of life—suffering is part of life. It cannot be removed. Each person must find his own way of escape and not worry about other people. Contrast this with the Christian view. Five hundred twenty years after the death of Buddha, Jesus appeared to bring full and abundant life, not only in the world to come, but in this world. Buddha claimed to have found a way, but Jesus claimed that He is *the* way. How do these two claims compare? Let's look at the teachings of Buddha against those of the Bible.

Comparing Buddha's teachings with the Bible

Buddha said that "to live is to suffer," but he gave no reason for suffering. The Bible agrees that suffering is everywhere, but it provides an explanation for suffering.

Romans 8:18-23 says that the entire world "groans" and that all men suffer because of sin. Romans 5 tells us that when Adam sinned, he infected the entire bloodstream of humanity with sickness and suffering and death. The Bible also declares men are sinners by choice. In the biblical view, sin is basically rebellion against God.

Buddha correctly observed that suffering comes from a desire for the things of the world. Christians call these desires temptation.

James 1:13-15 points out that a man is enticed from

within, by "evil desires," "lusts," and passions or appetites which tend to get out of control. When a person yields to these temptations, he sins. The result of sin is spiritual suffering and death (see Rom. 6:23).

Christians agree that the cause of suffering is selfish desire, but they disagree with the Buddhist way of removing this desire.

Buddha taught that the only way to rid oneself of selfish desire was through self-effort. For centuries his followers have tried to stay on the Eightfold Path, but many have found that "the heart is deceitful above all things. . . and beyond cure. Who can stand it?" (Jer. 17:9) and will sabotage the best of human intentions.

For a person to master himself, he must have a higher source of strength. But Buddha is agnostic. He ignores the possibility of help from God. The apostle Paul (see Titus 3:3-8) reminds us that every Christian was once a slave to desire, to all sorts of selfish hungers, but that Christ came into the world as God and as man to supply the strength to overcome these desires. Without the help of God the only way to end desire is to die. But with God, we can become "new creatures" who die (figuratively) to selfish desires. (Also see John 3:5; 2 Cor. 5:17; Gal. 2:20.)

Buddha said that to end desire one must follow the Eightfold Path: right viewpoint, aspiration, speech, behavior, occupation, effort, mindfulness, meditation. These noble ideas are much like those taught by Jesus in the Sermon on the Mount.

How Christianity goes beyond Buddhism

The problem with Buddhism is that its goals are beyond man's ability to reach. Jesus set the same kind of standards, but He also gives strength to live a life that is pleasing to God.

Christ shares in the life of the true believer. On the night before He was crucified, Jesus gave His disciples a perfect illustration of how to be a successful Christian. He compared Himself to a grapevine and His followers to the grapevine's branches, because He knew His disciples would be familiar with a plant that grew all over Palestine. It might be easier for people today to picture a rose bush, or a fruit tree, but the analogy is the same.

Jesus said: "You [the branches] must go on growing in me [the vine or main trunk]. . . . It is the man who shares my life and whose life I share who proves fruitful. For the plain fact is that apart from me you can do nothing at all. The man who does not share my life is like a branch that is broken off and withers away. He becomes just like the dry sticks that men pick up and use for firewood. But if you live your life in me, and my words live in your hearts, you can ask for whatever you like and it will come true for you" (John 15:4-7, *Phillips*).

And Jesus went on to say: "You must go on living in my love. If you keep my commandments you will live in my love just as I have kept my Father's commandments and live in his love" (vv. 9,10).

Jesus Christ gives His followers two vital ingredients for effective living: power and authority. The Christian increases or limits that power in direct proportion to how much of his life he really shares with his Lord and how obedient he is to his Lord.

The choice every man must make

Christ does not simply give the Christian a list of commandments and orders to obey. He promises to help the Christian grow and change and develop, just as a vine, a bush, or a tree grows under proper care. The Buddhist on the other hand has eight guidelines for the right way to live, but Buddha promises him no power to live that way. And Buddha has no real authority for saying these eight steps are right, noble as these eight steps may sound. Christ says "I am the way" (John 14:6) and He proved His power and authority by rising from the dead. That same power and authority is available to Christians, but many Christians never fully realize what Christ can do for them because they don't really live their lives in Him.

Buddha taught: "You yourself must make the effort." Christ teaches: "Turn yourself over to me and I will give you power to live successfully."

Every man, Christian or otherwise, faces this choice: self-effort or yielding everything to Christ as Saviour *and* Lord. When Christians accept Christ only as a Saviour, but fail to obey Him as Lord, they shortchange themselves and in some respects are no better off than the Buddhist who grapples with craving (selfish desire) in his own strength. Perhaps a lesson the Christian can learn from the Buddhist is to recognize that even though he is "saved through faith in Christ" there is still craving (selfish desire) in his life. That craving is there because he has not turned everything over to the One who has plainly said, "Without me (without living all of your life in me) you can do nothing." The Christian must make Christ Lord of his life.

What's the difference?

Christians	*Buddhists*
GOD	
God is Omniscient and Omnipotent (Job 42:2; Ps. 115:3; Matt. 19:26).	Deny existence of a personal God.
JESUS CHRIST	
He is the unique Son of God who died for men's sin (Matt. 14:33; 16:16; John 1:34; 9:35-37; 1 Cor. 15:3; Rom. 5:6-8).	He was a good teacher, less important than Buddha.

SIN

Sin is any thought or deed contrary to the will of God. Man is spiritually dead in sin (Rom. 3:10,23; 5:12; Eph. 2:1).

Sin is anything which hinders man's progress. Man is responsible for his own sin.

SALVATION

Salvation is through Christ's efforts only (Acts 4:12; Titus 3:5; Eph. 2:8-10).

Man is saved by self-effort only.

For Further Reading

Smith, Huston. *Religions of Man*. New York: Harper and Row Publishers, Inc., 1965.

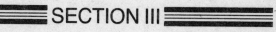

SECTION III

MAJOR CULTS

UNITARIANISM
"We are not bound by a particular book—the Bible, or a particular person—even Jesus"—Dana McLean Greeley.

JEHOVAH'S WITNESSES
"Christ came to the kingdom in 1914, but unseen by men"—*The Truth Will Make You Free*.

CHRISTIAN SCIENCE
"God is all, therefore matter is nothing beyond an image in mortal mind"—Mary Baker Eddy.

MORMONISM
"God himself was once as we are now and is an exalted man"—Joseph Smith.

===== 9 =====
Unitarianism
Flat Denial of All Orthodox Doctrines

King Solomon once wrote that "there is nothing new under the sun" (Eccles. 1:9). In the case of today's cults, there is no new heresy they have invented. From the first century A.D. to the present, men have belonged to groups which deny that Jesus was exactly who He said He was and did exactly what He said He would do.

But what is a cult? What do its members believe? Webster defines a cult as "a religion regarded as unorthodox or spurious; also a minority religious group holding beliefs regarded as unorthodox or spurious."[1] So a cult is an organization that has broken away from orthodoxy, or has been organized to oppose orthodoxy.

Many cults have come and gone since the time of Christ. Their names are only found in theology books. Their beliefs are studied only by scholars. No doubt the cults we know today will someday be historical curiosities, but since they do exist in our time, we must know what they teach.

What makes a cult a cult?

Most cults generally hold these views in common:

• Cultists believe that all Christian churches are wrong and that their cult is a special group that has the real truth about God.

• Cultists attack the deity of Jesus Christ and either lower Him to the level of man or raise man to the level of Christ.

• Cultists deny that man can be saved by faith in Christ alone. They teach that man can make himself right with God by good works and by obeying the teachings of the cult.

• Cultists believe the statements of their leaders who claim to have new interpretations of the Bible, or valuable additions to it.

• Many cults claim to believe the Bible, but they distort its teachings to suit their own particular beliefs about man, God, the Holy Spirit, heaven and hell, salvation and other vital doctrines.

A small cult with a wide influence

Solomon's statement that there is nothing new under the sun holds true for Unitarians, a cult small in numbers, but wide in influence. Unitarians like to think of themselves as modern and progressive, but their beliefs go back into antiquity.

The first Unitarians were a group known as Monarchians. They were prominent from the middle of the second century to the end of the third century. They held that there is no such thing as the Trinity: Father, Son and Holy Spirit. They insisted that God is one and that He cannot manifest Himself into three persons.

In the fourth century, a Greek scholar of North Africa suddenly leaped into prominence. His name was Arius and he began to teach that there is no such thing as the Trinity. Controversy became so heated that the Roman emperor, Constantine I, called a council of church officials and theologians to study the question. Their findings, based in large part on biblical evidence, were reported in the document called the Nicene Creed. It states that Father, Son, and Holy Spirit are all of "one substance." Despite the Nicene Creed, Unitarianism has continued to infect the bloodstream of the church.

From the sixteenth to the seventeenth century, Unitarian churches were prominent in Poland. It was also popular in seventeenth century England, during the reign of James I.

The rise of Unitarianism in America

In America, Unitarianism became important early in the eighteenth century. It developed mainly as a reaction against the rigid Calvinism of the New England Congregational churches. John Calvin, the French theologian, strongly influenced Congregationalists, Presbyterians, and other Protestant groups.

During the eighteenth century, Unitarianism gained two great leaders, Jonathan Mayhew and Charles Chauncey, who were deeply involved in the operation of Harvard College. They helped to change Harvard from its original Christian position to Unitarianism.

Another leader, William Ellery Channing, a clergyman who died in 1842, has been called the "Apostle of Unitarianism." Channing was spokesman for those New England Protestants who rejected Calvinist doctrines of predestination and the sinfulness of man. In a sermon delivered in 1819, he stated the basic beliefs of Unitarianism. This led to the formation in 1825 of the American Unitarian Association.

There were and are several groups of Unitarians. One group, for instance, believed that while Jesus wasn't exactly God, He wasn't exactly mere man, either. Another group, founded by the New England poet and essayist Ralph Waldo Emerson, believed that everything in nature, even man, was part of a great Oversoul. Another group got deeply interested in the writings of German theologians who tried to prove that the Bible is not the Word of God.

Today, these groups are loosely united by the Unitarian Universalist Association which merged in 1961. Over a quarter of a million people now consider themselves Unitarians.

Unitarianism a foundation for liberal theology

There are many other people who are not Unitarians but hold similar views. Those who remain in Christian churches while holding these views are called "liberals."

Unitarians and liberals agree on certain key points:

They do not believe that the Bible is the Word of God. Some of them say parts of it may contain the Word of God mixed with superstition.

They not only deny that the Bible is the Word of God, but also *deny the Christian doctrines that are derived from it.*

They do not think that God is a person. They think of Him as a Force, an Oversoul, a Prime Mover, or even as being dead!

They think of Jesus as merely a man, an exceptional man like Moses and Buddha, but no more than a man. In their view Jesus' main contribution was as a teacher.

Their theology constantly changes. Dr. Dana McLean Greeley, a former president of the Unitarians, put it this way, "Actually we Unitarians are changing all the time. And we are not bound by adherence to a particular book—the Bible—or a particular person—even Jesus—or a particular city as a place of our birth and authority, neither Rome nor Mecca nor Boston."[2]

They believe that man should not look to God for help, but should be his own savior. A Unitarian minister, the Reverend Carl M. Chorowsky, stated their position of salvation this way:

"Unitarians recognize evil and man's responsibility for much of it. . . Because of the total depravity of man, supposedly, God sent His only begotten Son to the world to die for sinful men. Such doctrine Unitarians find offensive, unbiblical, even immoral. It is certainly inconsistent with the nature of God or the dignity of man, whom the Eternal One created in the image of God, to love with an everlasting love."[3]

The idea of hell insults Unitarians

Unitarians do not believe that man is a sinner. They think he is only imperfect and say that all he needs is "redemption of character." In other words, all that's required is to lead a good life and follow the Golden Rule.

In his sermon, "Instant Unitarianism," the Reverend Stephen H. Fritchman expands on this idea:

"Contemporary Unitarians believe that each man must achieve his own salvation, or life pattern, by his own thinking and effort. . . Few Unitarians today are motivated by a rewards and punishment theory, as were some of their ancestors. The good life is immediately self-validating. Fear of hell or the promises of heaven play almost no part in the Unitarian's life today."[4]

Or, to quote Dr. Greeley again, "From a Unitarian point of view, there is no heaven or hell. Theologically such an idea is repulsive and unacceptable in the light of the moral affirmation of man."[5]

Clearly then, since there's no hell, there's no need of salvation through Jesus Christ. The very idea of hell is an insult to the goodness of man.

Consider Dr. Greeley's statement after the merger of the Unitarians and the Universalists (who hold similar views): "The old saw says the difference between the Unitarians and Universalists is that the Universalists thought that God was too good to damn man and that the Unitarians thought man was too good to be damned. That epitomizes the theological origins of both."[6]

Unitarianism is another name for humanism

This side of Unitarianism, the glorification of man, has come to be called humanism. Humanism, often called "the fourth faith," is found in most of our schools, colleges, universities, and in many of our churches.

The term "humanism" was popularized with the publication in 1933 of "A Humanist Manifesto." The authors were 33 well-known men who were Unitarians, liberal churchmen, and atheists.[7]

The main point of the manifesto is that man is his own master, and that he is basically good. The first statement of the manifesto reads: "Religious humanists regard the universe as self-existing and not created." So they begin by denying the creative activity of God. Some other statements: "Humanism asserts that the nature of the universe depicted by modern science makes unacceptable any supernatural or cosmic guarantees of human values," and, "There will be no uniquely religious emotions and attitudes of the kind hitherto associated with belief in the supernatural."

Every cult has a weak link, and Unitarianism is no exception. Their opinion that man is basically good and steadily improving is easily refuted. Even a casual study of history (both ancient and modern) shows that much of man's "progress" has been written with blood. A casual glance at today's newspaper shows that there is terrible evil in man and in every nation.

How Freud helps refute Unitarianism

Both Unitarians and Protestant liberals teach that education is the answer to man's individual and national problems. But Sigmund Freud, though an atheist, once declared, "The more civilized man becomes, the more neurotic he becomes." Look around and judge for yourself if that statement is true.

The desire to get rid of God and glorify man is not new.

Paul indicts this desire as the cause of all man's troubles and sinful actions (see Rom. 1:18-32). Paul says that from the beginning:

"They knew all the time that there is a God, yet they refused to acknowledge him as such, or to thank him for what he is or does. Thus they became fatuous in their argumentations, and plunged their silly minds still further into the dark. Behind a facade of 'wisdom' they became just fools, fools who would exchange the glory of the immortal God for an image of a mortal man, or of creatures that run or fly or crawl. They gave up God: and therefore God gave them up—to be the playthings of their own foul desires in dishonoring their own bodies.

"These men deliberately forfeited the truth of God and accepted a lie, paying homage and giving service to the creature instead of to the Creator, who alone is worthy to be worshiped for ever and ever, amen" (Rom. 1:21-25, *Phillips*).

Man's moral record refutes Unitarianism

Man has done marvelous things in science and technology. Yet Elton Trueblood, the Quaker scholar, has written, "Just at the moment of history when the technical conditions for the oneness of the globe have finally appeared, we are woefully lacking in the moral conditions that are required if this situation is to be a blessings."[8]

If the Unitarians are right and education is all that is needed to improve man, then the Nazis of Germany should have been moral supermen. But the result when man's evil nature is unrestrained is a matter of gruesome record.

Let's be realistic and honest. Man today is in a moral predicament from which he cannot drag himself. Where can we turn for help? The most logical place is the Bible, the very book Unitarians and liberals try so hard to discredit. Isn't it likely that there's something vital and exciting in a book that requires so much time and trouble to prove wrong?

If we look, we won't be disappointed. The Bible is an excellent source of information on the subject of man. The Bible has more to say about man than any book on psychology or sociology that has ever been written.

First, the Bible points out man's great failing, his pride. Solomon wrote, "Pride only breeds quarrels" (Prov. 13:10). James also hit the nail on the head when he indicted greed as a man's source of trouble in the world:

"What causes fights and quarrels among you? Don't they come from your desires that battle within you? You want something but don't get it. You kill and covet, but you cannot have what you want. You quarrel and fight. You do not have, because you do not ask God. When you ask, you do not receive, because you ask with wrong motives, that you may spend what you get on your pleasures" (Jas. 4:1-3).

The choice: trust man or God

The Bible points out that man is not reliable. The Unitarian wants us to put our trust in mankind, but the Bible warns, "It is better to take refuge in the Lord than to trust in man" (Ps. 118:8). Solomon also wrote, "Many a man claims to have unfailing love, but a faithful man who can find? Who can say, 'I have kept my heart pure; I am clean and without sin'?" (Prov. 20:6,9).

The Bible also emphasizes the fact that man is mortal. When God broke the pride of Solomon, the king wrote, "Man's fate is like that of the animals; the same fate awaits them both: As one dies, so dies the other. All have the same breath; man has no advantage over the animal. Everything is meaningless" (Eccles. 3:19).

What is the way out of man's predicament? Should man ignore the evidence of what he is and accept the claims of Dr. Greeley?

"Unitarianism or a creed like it is definitely the wave of

the future in a democratic society. I'm not sure whether it will be under our name, but, combining the scientific spirit and an adventurous faith, it will sweep the world.''9

Or should he listen to Solomon?

''Now all has been heard; here is the conclusion of the matter: Fear God and keep his commandments, for this is the whole duty of man. For God will bring every deed into judgment, including every hidden thing, whether it is good or evil'' (Eccles. 12:13,14).

Or to Paul?

''Therefore, if anyone is in Christ, he is a new creation; the old has gone, the new has come!'' (2 Cor. 5:17).

Man wants to change. How can he change? He is offered on one hand the answer of the Unitarians, liberals and humanists, and on the other hand the claims of Jesus Christ.

Which answer will he accept? The immediate destiny of mankind and the individual's eternal destiny may hang in the balance.

What's the difference?

Christians	*Unitarians*
GOD	
God is revealed in the Scriptures as Father, Son and Holy Spirit—the Trinity (Matt. 3:13-17; 28:19; 2 Cor. 13:14).	''God is one.'' They deny the doctrine of the Trinity. They also deny that God is a personal deity and use the term ''God'' to refer to the living processes of nature and conscience at work in mankind.
THE BIBLE	
The Bible is divinely inspired and is their sole guide and authority for faith (2 Tim.	The Bible is a collection of ''myths and legends'' and philosophical writings. They

3:15-17; 2 Pet. 1:19-21; 1 Thess. 2:13).	deny the authority and accuracy of the Scriptures.

JESUS CHRIST

Christ is divine, a part of the Trinity—God Himself. Christ Himself frequently referred to Himself as God (John 8:58; 8:12-30).	Jesus was no more or less divine than any man. They deny the doctrine of the Trinity as well as the deity of Christ.

SIN

Man is inherently sinful and there is only one way man can rid himself of his sinful nature—through faith by the grace (unmerited love) of God (Eph. 2:8,9; 4:20-24).	Man is essentially good and he can save himself by improvement—"redemption of character."

Notes

1. *Webster's Third New International Dictionary*.

2. Dana McLean Greeley, "Spry Downgrader of Divinity," *Life* magazine (July 28, 1967), p. 31.

3. "What Is a Unitarian?" *Look* magazine (March 8, 1955).

4. Stephen H. Fritchman, *Sermon of the Month* (Los Angeles: First Unitarian Church).

5. Greeley, *Life*, p. 35.

6. Ibid.

7. Wilbur M. Smith, *Therefore Stand* (Hollistan, MA: Wilde Company, 1945), pp. 67-70.

8. Elton Trueblood, *The Predicament of Modern Man* (New York: Harper and Row Publishers, Inc., 1944), p. 14.

9. Greeley, *Life*, p. 31.

For Further Reading

Martin, Walter R. *The Kingdom of the Cults*. Grand Rapids: Zondervan Publishing House, 1965.

Lewis, Gordon R. *Confronting the Cults*. Philadelphia: Presbyterian and Reformed Publishing Company, 1966.

Robertson, Irvine. *What the Cults Believe*. Chicago: Moody Press, 1966.

10
Jehovah's Witnesses
There Is No Hell; Hard Work Earns Heaven

When we first wrote this book we stated, "As cults go, Jehovah's Witnesses are a small group. They claim about a quarter of a million members in the United States." At this writing, about 14 years later, Jehovah's Witnesses have increased their number to one-half million in the United States and more than two-and-a-quarter million in the entire world.

Jehovah's Witnesses are a challenge to Christians for several reasons: (1) Most of their growth has taken place just recently; (2) they will probably continue growing because they preach their message to a world on the brink of nuclear war; (3) their teachings are flatly opposed to the gospel; (4) they are flatly opposed to the Christian church which they say is of the devil; (5) they deny the deity of Jesus Christ, the person and work of the Holy Spirit and many other vital doctrines; and (6) they claim that their teachings are the only real truth about the Bible.

This should be enough to interest the Christian in learning about the dangerous teachings of this cult. Yet few Christians know much about these ardent doorbell ringers who come armed with literature and Scripture verses.

History of the Jehovah's Witnesses

Charles Taze Russell is the official founder of the group. He was born in 1852 in Allegheny, Pennsylvania. As a youth, he developed a terrible fear of hell. It was said that he often went around writing on sidewalks to warn people about hell-fire.

At the age of 17 Russell got into a long discussion with a person who denied the existence of hell. He wound up convinced that this person was right.

Another turning point came at the age of 18; he wandered into a church where the second coming of Christ was being discussed. He got interested in just when Christ was to come again. To solve the problem, he began to study the Bible. Very soon he published his findings in a pamphlet entitled *The Object and Manner of the Lord's Return*.

For centuries, great minds of the church have wrestled with the problem of the Second Coming, but Russell felt that he had solved it in almost no time at all.

Russell's pamphlet consists of a lengthy, complicated, and incorrect interpretation of unrelated Scriptures combined with an intricate method of computing time. The end result of his labors was the statement that Jesus Christ would return in 1874. Later, Russell changed the date to 1914. This return was not to be a physical one, but a spiritual one. In other words, when Christ would return, He would not be seen. This of course contradicts Revelation 1:7. Much of the teaching of the Witnesses revolves around Russell's views of the Second Coming.

In 1874, Russell was elected pastor of a Bible class that he had been teaching for four years. This marked the real beginning of the cult, for this was the year of Christ's supposed return and he was the leader of the group to whom Christ would be revealed.

In 1879, Russell began to publish the magazine, *Zion's Watchtower and Herald of Christ's Presence*. This proved helpful in expanding the movement. By 1880 there were 30 new congregations in seven states. By 1881, Zion's Watchtower and Tract Society was established, and it was chartered in 1884. The Jehovah's Witness movement was now official.

Russell married Maria Frances Ackley in 1879. He appointed her secretary-treasurer of the society and associate editor of the *Watchtower*. Through the years she became bitterly disappointed at the way her articles were treated by her husband. Jehovah's Witnesses claim that this is why she eventually left both the society and her husband. In 1913 Mrs. Russell sued her husband for divorce on the grounds of "his conceit, egotism, domination, and improper conduct to other women."[1]

In June, 1912, Rev. J.J. Ross, a Baptist pastor of Hamilton, Ontario, denounced Russell in a pamphlet. At once, Russell sued Ross. On the witness stand, Russell was caught in at least one lie. He was asked whether he knew Greek, the original language of the New Testament. "Oh, yes," he answered. But when asked to read some Greek letters, he admitted that he had not told the truth.[2]

Russell had claimed to be an ordained minister, but under oath he admitted that he had never been ordained by anyone.[3] Such willful perjury reflects badly on a man who claimed to have the one and only interpretation of God's Word. Jehovah's Witnesses now claim that they don't believe Russell's teachings, but close examination of their writings refutes that claim.

When Russell died in 1916, Joseph Franklin Rutherford, known as "Judge" Rutherford, was elected leader of the cult. Under Rutherford, the organization grew by leaps and bounds.

Rutherford set up headquarters in Brooklyn, New York. Though an able administrator, Rutherford had his problems with the law. In May, 1918, Rutherford, along with eight other leaders of the society, was arrested for "conspiring to cause insubordination and refusal of duty in United States military and naval forces.''[4] On June 20, they were found guilty and were sentenced to 20 years in the federal penitentiary. However, in May, 1919, they were set free because of petitions sent to the government by the Witnesses.[5]

This trial of Rutherford did not discourage the Witnesses, for in the Second World War 3,500 Witnesses were imprisoned for refusing military service. Witnesses also refuse to pledge allegiance to the flag, or to follow any government laws because Rutherford taught that all human government is of the devil.

The Brooklyn office, closed during the trial and imprisonment of Rutherford and his executives, reopened on October 1, 1919 and is going strong today.

Rutherford died on January 8, 1942 and Nathan Homer Knorr was elected to be the society's third president. Knorr was born in Bethlehem, Pennsylvania, in 1905, became a full-time Jehovah's Witness at 18, joining the headquarters staff in Brooklyn. From there he went straight to the top.

Knorr was not much like the first two leaders. He shunned publicity; his name rarely appeared in newspapers. Under his leadership new emphasis was placed on training programs for Witnesses. Also they published a translation of the Bible that conforms more to the doctrines of the society, *The New World Translation of the Christian Scriptures*. The translators of this "Bible" remain anonymous. Most Bible scholars are glad to sign their work, but the Witnesses today rarely reveal the authors of their writings.

Under Knorr's direction, the work of the Jehovah's Witnesses spread not only in this country, but also in 185 other countries in the world.

The teachings of the Jehovah's Witnesses

Jehovah's Witnesses are well known for their witnessing on street corners and door to door. Why do Jehovah's Witnesses witness so much? They witness because they are working hard to earn their salvation. Since Jehovah's Witnesses do not believe in hell they have no fear of eternal punishment, but they do fear that they will not meet Jehovah's standards for salvation. Russell denied the existence of hell, but he substituted a terror of God.

Why does a Jehovah's Witness witness so much? His motive is not love of God, but rather a dreadful terror of God. Russell denied the existence of hell, but he substituted something that seems much more terrible—death of the soul as well as the body.

Jesus often spoke of hell. He called it "Gehenna," the place of torment. (See Matt. 5:22,29,30; 10:28; 18:9; 23:15,33.) Revelation 19:20 and 20:10,14,15 describes a "lake of fire."

Russell could not accept this. He argued that it is unreasonable and contrary to God's love. In place of hell, he invented the doctrine of annihilation which states that a person's soul dies when his body dies. He taught that a person could escape this fate only by accepting and preaching the doctrines of the Jehovah's Witnesses.

The organization is divided into two main groups, but there are minor ones as well. Those who hold important offices and make major decisions are called the 144,000. This number comes from Revelation 7:4-8 which most Christians interpret as a symbolic number referring to the 12 tribes of Israel. Jehovah's Witnesses say that this text speaks of 144,000 Witnesses who have been chosen by God to be special leaders.

The rest of the group, those who come door to door, are called the "other sheep," or Jonadabs. Jonadabs do not have the same eternal future as the 144,000 and they must work hard to earn their salvation. This is the reason they are so zealous and dedicated.

The teachings of the Witnesses point to a great occurrence

that they say will take place sometime soon—the Battle of Armageddon. In the Bible, this refers to the last great battle against Israel (see Rev. 16:16). But the Witnesses, in their typical freewheeling interpretation, claim that Armageddon will be worldwide, thermonuclear devastation.

According to the Witnesses, on one side will be all the nations of the world, the leaders of Christianity (who they say are of the devil), and all the heathen. On the other side will be those of the 144,000 who are still alive and the "other sheep." Besides the battle on earth, there will be a battle in heaven between God and Satan. Jehovah's Witnesses won't have to fight; Jehovah Himself will do the fighting for them.

The result of the battle will be terrible. Over two billion people will die, all of Christianity will be wiped out, and all the nations will be destroyed. Not one person who was against Jehovah and His Witnesses will remain alive. Only faithful Witnesses will survive Armageddon.

During the next thousand years after Armageddon, many good things will happen to the Witnesses. First, as the remnant of the 144,000 (who are still on earth after Armageddon) die they will go immediately to heaven to reign with Jesus. The "other sheep," survivors of the great battle, will clean up the debris and get ready for the great judgments to come.

Next, multitudes will be brought back to life. Great personalities will be "resurrected," such as Abraham, Moses, and David.

Jehovah's Witnesses say that after the Old Testament heroes have been brought back, then the "other sheep" will be raised. Next, Jehovah will "recreate" all the people who never had a chance to hear the truth about Jehovah. The rest will remain annihilated. During the thousand years, these billions of people will be "educated." On the day of judgment, they will choose whether to accept or reject Jehovah. Those who reject Jehovah will be annihilated. The rest will remain on earth forever.

JEHOVAH'S WITNESSES SYSTEM OF SALVATION

"Saved" are divided into two classes:

THE ANOINTED CLASS ... 144,000 chosen by God to rule in heaven with Christ. Sometimes called the "little flock."

THE OTHER SHEEP ... the many other believers who earn eternal life on earth.

UNSAVED face non-existence .. Jehovah's Witnesses do not believe in hell or eternal punishment.

Man faces four possible destinies:

1. HEAVEN
The anointed class—144,000—reign eternally with Christ.

2. RENEWED EARTH
After Armageddon and the Millennium, all those who please Jehovah will enjoy eternal life on an Eden-like earth.

NON-EXISTENCE

3. All wicked dead who die without chance of resurrection or opportunity to work for salvation during millenium.

4. All of those who fail to pass Millenial tests are annihilated.

Jehovah's Witnesses set dates for prophesied events.

1914—Kingdom of God began with return of Christ's presence. Many of 144,000 now reign in heaven with Christ.

1975—End of 6th 1000-year-day of man's existence. Probable date of Armaggedon (in early autumn).

2075—End of 7th 1000-year-day of man's existence. Early autumn, probable time of the close of the millennium, people judged and given eternal life on renewed earth or annihilation.

Is any of this in the Bible?

Not at all. Nowhere does the Bible teach that anyone will have a second chance before the day of judgment. First Corinthians 15 says that only those who believe in Jesus Christ will be raised at His return and that only those who believe and are alive at the time of His return will be taken by Him into heaven. Revelation 20 says that after Christ has reigned for a thousand years, those who were not Christians will be raised and judged according to their works. There's no mention of any "educational period" during this time. Revelation 20:15 makes it very clear, however, that "if anyone's name was not found written in the book of life, he was thrown into the lake of fire."

One thing that makes Jehovah's Witnesses unique is their bitter hatred for Christianity. They relish the idea of all Christians being destroyed in Armageddon. They have also devised a fanciful myth about Christ.

The Witnesses teach that Christ is not equal to God, but that He was *created* by God. For them, Jehovah is the only Saviour. When Christ lived in heaven, they say, He was known as the angel Michael. However, when Christ came to earth, He was stripped of His angelic nature and became only a man.

So it was only as a man that Jesus died on the cross and a man's death is not enough to atone for the sins of the world. The Witnesses also teach that Jesus was not bodily resurrected, but only as a spirit. However, like others who have said this, the Witnesses cannot explain what happened to Christ's body. For them like many other doubters, the empty tomb with the unwrapped grave clothes (see John 20:5) is an unsolvable mystery.

To be able to face the claims of the Witnesses, the Christian must be absolutely sure of his salvation based on the crucifixion and resurrection of Christ. He must say with Paul, "Now if the rising of Christ from the dead is the very heart of our message, how can some of you deny that there is any resurrection?. . . if Christ did not rise your faith is futile and your sins have never been forgiven. Moreover those who have died believing in Christ are utterly dead and gone. . . . But the glorious fact is that Christ was raised from the dead'' (1 Cor. 15:12,16,17,20, *Phillips*).

And it is on this wonderful fact that our faith and our hope of eternal life is grounded.

What's the difference?

Christians	*Jehovah's Witnesses*
GOD	
God is eternal, personal, spiritual Being in three persons—the Trinity: Father, Son and Holy Spirit (Matt. 3:13-17; 28:19; 2 Cor. 13:14).	There is one solitary being from all eternity, Jehovah God, the Creator and Preserver of the Universe and all things. They deny the doctrine of the Trinity.
IMMORTALITY	
Scripture teaches that man has an eternal, immortal soul (Gen. 1:26; 5:1; Job 32:8; Acts 7:59; 1 Cor. 11:7).	Man does not have an immortal soul. They teach that the soul is not separate from the body.
JESUS CHRIST	
Christ is divine, a part of the Trinity, God Himself (John 1:1; Col. 1:15-19; 2:9; 1 John 5:7,8).	Christ was not God but God's first created creature. They deny Christ's deity.
ATONEMENT	
Christ's death was the complete payment for man's sins (Rom. 3:24,25; Col. 1:20;	Christ's death provides the opportunity for man to work for his salvation: perfect hu-

1 Pet. 2:24; 2 Cor. 5:20).	man life for eternity on an Eden-like earth.

CHRIST'S RESURRECTION

Christ was bodily resurrected from the grave (John 2:21; 20:24-29; Luke 24:36-43).	Christ was raised a "divine spirit." They deny the bodily resurrection of Christ.

CHRIST'S RETURN

Christ will return to earth physically (1 Thess. 4:16,17; Matt. 24:30; Zech. 12:10; Rev. 1:7).	Christ returned to earth— invisibly—in 1914 and now rules earth from heaven.

HELL

There is eternal punishment for sin (Matt. 5:22; 8:11,12; 13:42,50; 22:13; Luke 13:24-28; 2 Pet. 2:17; Jude 13; Rev. 14:9-11).	There is no hell or eternal punishment. Those who do not measure up to Jehovah's standards will be annihilated, meaning they will be or know no more.

Notes

1. Anthony Hoekema, *The Four Major Cults* (Grand Rapids: Wm. B. Eerdmans Publishing Company, 1963), p. 227, note 12.
2. Ibid.
3. Ibid., pp. 227,228.
4. Ibid., p. 229.
5. Ibid.

For Further Reading

Bjornstad, James. *Counterfeits at Your Door*. Glendale, CA: Regal Books, 1979.
Dencher, Ted. *The Watchtower Versus the Bible*. Chicago: Moody Press, 1961.
From Paradise Lost to Paradise Regained. Brooklyn: Watchtower Bible and Tract Society, 1958.
Gruss, Edmond Charles. *Apostles of Denial*. Nutley, NJ: Presbyterian and Reformed Publishing Company, 1970.

Kern, Herbert. *How to Respond to Jehovah's Witnesses*. St. Louis: Concordia Publishing House, 1977.

Lewis, Gordon. *Confronting the Cults*. Philadelphia: Presbyterian and Reformed Publishing Company, 1966.

Robertson, Irvine. *What the Cults Believe*. Chicago: Moody Press, 1966.

Schnell, William J. *How to Witness to Jehovah's Witnesses*. Grand Rapids: Baker Books, 1975.

_____ *Jehovah's Witnesses Errors Exposed*. Grand Rapids: Baker Books, 1978.

═══ 11 ═══
Christian Science
Denies Reality but Cannot Escape It

"God is all-in-all.

"God is good. Good is Mind.

"God, Spirit, being all, nothing is matter.

"Life, God, omnipotent good, deny death, evil, sin, disease.—Disease, sin, evil, death, deny good, omnipotent God, Life."[1]

These cryptic phrases, more like the mystic Hinduism than straightforward Christianity, are the basic teachings of Christian Science. Simply stated, if such peculiar language can be simply stated, they mean the following:

1. God is in everything and is everything.

2. God is good and all that is good is Mind.

3. Because God is Mind (or Spirit), everything that is not Spirit does not exist. Matter is not Spirit, so it does not exist.

4. Therefore, material things such as disease, sin, death, and evil do not exist. Only that which is good actually exists.

Mary Baker Eddy's early life

This is the thinking revealed in the writings of Mary Baker Eddy, founder of Christian Science.

Mary Baker was born into a stern Calvinist New Hampshire family on July 16, 1821. Her father, Mark Baker, held strictly to the teachings of John Calvin, especially on such matters as final judgment day, the wrath of God toward sinners, eternal punishment for unbelievers. Mary argued bitterly with her father on these issues, and this set the pattern for her later rejection of orthodox Christian teaching.

Mary was often ill as a child, so she missed much schooling. Her education came mostly through her own efforts.[2] When she was 22, she married George Glover, but after only six months he died. Mary soon gave birth to their son, whom she named George.

Ten years later, she married Daniel Patterson, a dentist. Patterson was said to have been unfaithful to Mary. After 13 years they separated and some years later they divorced.

Physical and mental suffering dominated Mary's life. Perhaps this is why, in 1862, she became intrigued with reports about a faith healer, one Phineas Quimby of Portland, Maine.

Mary went to consult Quimby, then reported herself cured. She became an ardent disciple. She tried to use Quimby's methods on others. His technique involved hypnotism and laying on hands. Mary was convinced that Quimby had rediscovered the healing method of Jesus. She even gave a lecture on the subject.

But Mary soon lost interest in Quimby. She had begun to launch a healing career of her own. She denied that she owed any of her technique to Quimby. But others have disagreed.

Dr. Quimby's contribution to Christian Science

In spite of the official view of the Christian Science church, many who have studied the question say that she even copied large sections of his manuscript.[3] Certainly there are many similarities. Quimby described his system as "the Science of Christ," and Mrs. Eddy called hers "Christian

Science." Both Quimby and Mrs. Eddy described healing as opposing "truth to error." Both had similar ideas on the nonexistence of matter. Quimby had some knowledge of philosophy, but Mrs. Eddy was strictly an amateur, and she had a lot of trouble trying to explain this idea.

Shortly afer Quimby died, Mary (Mrs. Patterson at the time) slipped on an icy sidewalk and was painfully injured. She later claimed that this injury had been pronounced fatal by her doctor. Three days later, she picked up her Bible, opened it to Matthew 9:2-8 and read the account where Jesus healed the paralytic. At that point, she reported the healing truth dawned upon her, and she got up, fully cured.

However, there are a few disputed points in this account. Her doctor, Dr. Alvin M. Cushing, swore in an affidavit (Aug. 13, 1904) that he had never pronounced her critically ill and that she had never told him anything about a miraculous recovery.[4]

Despite all this, Mary Baker Eddy always maintained that the date of her healing (Feb. 1866) marked the beginning of Christian Science. She said this date coincided with the second coming of Christ.[5] This event was spiritual and invisible and was seen only in the founding of Christian Science.

Christian Science: 12 lessons for $300

By 1870, Mary was teaching her system (12 lessons for only $300). Her graduates set themselves up as healers and charged fees as high as any licensed medical doctor.

In 1875, Mary finished writing *Science and Health*. No publisher would take the book, so three of her associates helped get it into print.

In 1877, Mary married Asa Gilbert Eddy, a former student. He was the first to be granted the title, "Christian Science Practitioner."

The Church of Christ (Scientist) was incorporated on August 23, 1879. The headquarters were set up in Boston.

Naturally, Mrs. Eddy was the church's first pastor and dominated its leadership until her death.

Even after it was published, Mrs. Eddy continued to work on her book *Science and Health*. She gave her new manuscript to James Henry Wiggin, a retired Unitarian minister, and asked him to change a "few things here and there."[6]

Wiggin later reported his reaction in the *New York World* of November 6, 1906:

"The misspelling, capitalization and punctuation were dreadful, but these were not the things that fazed me. It was the thought and the general elemental arrangement of the work. There were passages that flatly and absolutely contradicted things that had preceded, and scattered all through were incorrect references to historical and philosophical matters.

". . . I was convinced that the only way in which I could undertake the requested revision would be to begin absolutely at the first page and rewrite the whole thing."[7]

The Bible errs, Christian Science is divine

Mrs. Eddy claimed in *Science and Health* that the Bible was her only "authority" and her only "textbook." She contradicts this claim, however, by stating that a Christian Scientist should use her book for a textbook because God was its author,[8] and because it is "the voice of Truth to this age, and contains the full statement of Christian Science."[9]

Furthermore, Mrs. Eddy stated that the Bible is in error in at least "three hundred thousand" places in the New Testament,[10] but on the other hand, Christian Science is "unerring and divine."[11] Mrs. Eddy also wrote that the historical parts of the Bible are unimportant. Only the spiritual parts are important.[12]

What does all this mean to a Christian Scientist? Simply this: *Science and Health,* the book so filled with errors and contradictions, is inspired and far superior to the Bible. Mrs.

Eddy claimed that the Bible is useful only when interpreted by *Science and Health*. Care to see a sample of how *Science and Health* interprets the Bible? Take the nature of man, for instance. Mrs. Eddy argued that Genesis, chapter one, is right and chapter two is wrong. She interpreted Genesis, chapter one, to mean that God created man as pure spirit:

"Man is not matter; he is not made up of brain, blood, bones, and other material elements. The Scriptures inform us that man is made in the image and likeness of God. Matter is not that likeness. . . Man is spiritual and perfect. . . He is. . . the reflection of God, or Mind, and therefore is eternal; that which has no separate mind from God; that which has not a single quality underived from Deity; that which possesses no life, intelligence, nor creative power of his own, but reflects spiritually all that belongs to his Maker."[13]

Therefore, she says, man is not sinful; his birth and death are just illusions, and because God is in everything, man is just like God. Of course, God can't be sick, so neither can man. Sickness, then, doesn't really exist, but is merely the imaginings of what she calls "Mortal Mind."

She holds Mortal Mind responsible for everything which *appears* to be bad in this *imaginary* world. But, she never bothers to explain what causes Mortal Mind. Her philosophy can't deal with the obvious embarrassing problem that if all things that exist are good because God is in them, then how can Mortal Mind, which is evil, exist?

Jesus Christ was never man, only Spirit

Another unfortunate effort at interpretation is the way she tried to define Jesus Christ according to Christian Science. She said that Jesus was not a real man, but only a spirit. To do this, she drew an artificial distinction between the two parts of His name, Jesus (His personal name) and Christ (His official name). She writes, "The spiritual Christ was infallible; Jesus, as material manhood, was not Christ."

As she tried to develop this, she got into hot water. She said, for example:

"The invisible Christ was imperceptible to the so-called personal senses, whereas Jesus appeared as a bodily existence. This dual personality of the unseen and the seen, the spiritual and material, the eternal Christ and the corporeal Jesus manifest in the flesh, continued until the Master's ascension."[14]

There are a good many problems here. First of all, though she denied the reality of the material world, she had to use words that everyone associates with the material world. She added "so-called" to "personal senses," but she forgot to qualify "bodily existence." This leads to another problem. If bodily existence is unreal, why bother with it? Why try to explain Jesus as visible and "manifest in the flesh," if the flesh itself is unreal? What difference does it make if Jesus appeared in the flesh if flesh does not exist?

Her evaluation of the person and the work of Jesus Christ are made clear in *Science and Health:*

"As a drop of water is one with the ocean, a ray of light one with the sun, even so God and man, Father and son, are one in being" (p. 361). In other words, Jesus is no different from other men because they are all part of God. This, of course, denies the deity of Christ.

"Jesus' students did not perform many wonderful works, until they saw him after his crucifixion and learned that he had not died" (pp. 45,46). Mrs. Eddy tried to solve the problem of the empty tomb like the Gnostics, who taught that Jesus was only a spirit, never a man, so He didn't really die nor rise from the dead. The apostle John wrote his Gospel to refute the Gnostics and it is also an effective answer for Christian Science.

"In his final demonstration, called the ascension, which closed the earthly record of Jesus, he arose above the physical knowledge of his disciples, and the material senses saw him no more'' (p. 46). Again, one must ask, what ''material senses''?

''The eternal Christ and the corporeal Jesus manifest in flesh, continued until the Master's ascension, when the human, material concept, or Jesus, disappeared'' (p. 334). In dealing with the problem of the empty tomb, Mrs. Eddy now resorts to an explanation used by the chief priests: ''You are to say, 'His disciples came during the night and stole him away while we were asleep' '' (Matt. 28:13).

''The material blood of Jesus was no more efficacious to cleanse from sin when it was shed upon 'the accursed tree,' than when it was flowing in his veins as he went daily about his Father's business'' (p. 25). Again we ask, what ''material blood,'' what ''sin,'' what ''business''? All of these things are of the material world, which in her view doesn't even exist.

These are just a few statements about Jesus Christ found in the sacred book of Christian Science, *Science and Health* by Mary Baker Eddy. Other statements deny the Trinity, the person of the Holy Spirit, the existence of sin, the need for salvation, the resurrection of the dead, final judgment, heaven and hell.

Christian Science: is it either?

Mrs. Eddy claimed that ''outside of Christian Science all is vague and hypothetical, the opposite of truth,''[15] but it's clear that she made a serious mistake in choosing the name ''Christian Science.'' Orthodox Christians find her anti-biblical statements far from the teachings of Christianity, while scientist cannot agree with Mrs. Eddy's denial of the reality of matter.

What did Christian Science do for Mrs. Eddy? According to E.F. Dakin in his book, *Mrs. Eddy: The Biography of a Virgin Mind,* she spent her old age in loneliness and in dreadful fear of ''malicious animal magnetism.'' She believed that people could wish harm on others, and she thought that her last husband, Mr. Eddy, died from arsenic "mentally administered." To ward off this evil, her followers were required to guard her bedroom door.

She trusted no one, became increasingly irritable. She could find no comfort in the book that she had written to explain the Christian Science approach to life. At 89, sad and alone, the reality of death closed in on Mary Baker Eddy who had, for so long, denied its very existence.

What's the difference?

Christians	*Christian Scientists*
GOD	
God is a Person. He created the universe, and created man in His own image (Gen. 1:1,26). God, as a Person, sees, hears, speaks, remembers, knows (Gen. 6:5; Exod. 2:24; Num. 11:1; Ps. 79:8; 2 Tim. 2:19).	God is an impersonal Principle, not a Person. Mrs. Eddy writes: "God is all . . . the soul, or mind, of the spiritual man is God, the Divine Principle of all being."
JESUS CHRIST	
Christ is one with God. Jesus said, "I and the Father are one" (John 10:30). Christians find much evidence of Christ's deity in the Scriptures: John 1:1; Phil. 2:5-8 and 1 John 2:22,23.	Jesus was not God. *Science and Health* states: "Jesus Christ is not God. . ." (p. 361). Scientists make Christ an outstanding man, a great teacher, but deny His deity.
MATTER	
What man sees, touches, feels, smells and hears is real. Jesus demonstrated the	Only Principle (God) exists and everything else is an "illusion." There is no mat-

reality of matter. He became flesh (John 1:14). He was hungry (Matt. 4:2). He gave others food to eat (Matt. 14:16).

"illusion." There is no matter; material things (a person's body, etc.) are not real.

SIN

Sin is real. It originates in the heart and mind of man, and separates man from God. The ultimate result of sin is death (Isa. 59:2; Mark 7:21-23; Rom. 5:12; 6:23).

Sin, evil and death do not exist. *Science and Health* states: Since God is All, there no room for the opposite . . . therefore evil, being the opposite of goodness, is unreal (p. 234).

THE ATONEMENT AND RESURRECTION

Christ's shed blood atoned for man's sins (1 Pet. 2:24) and Christ died and rose from the dead in bodily form (John 20:16,17,20,27).

Christ's shed blood on the cross did not cleanse man from sin and His disciples were fooled into thinking Him dead when He was really alive in the tomb (pp. 330 and 349, *Science and Health*).

Notes

1. Mary Baker Eddity, *Science and Health with Key to the Scriptures* (Boston: First Church of Christ Scientist), p. 113.

2. Sybil Wilbur, *The Life of Mary Baker Eddy* (Boston: The Christian Science Publishing Society, 1907), p. 21.

3. Anthony A. Hoekema, *Four Major Cults* (Grand Rapids: Wm. B. Eerdmans Publishing Co., 1963), p. 173.

4. Ernest S. Bates and John V. Dittemore, *Mary Baker Eddy: The Truth and the Tradition* (New York: Alfred A. Knopf, Inc., 1932), p. 112.

5. Mary Baker Eddy, *Retrospection and Introspection* (Boston: First Church of Christ Scientist), p. 78.

6. Edwin F. Dakin, *Mrs. Eddy* (New York: Charles Scribner's Sons, 1930), p. 225.

7. Bates, Dittemore, *Mary Baker Eddy*, p. 167.
8. Mary Baker Eddy, *First Church of Christ Scientist and Miscellany* (Boston: First Church of Christ Scientist), p. 115.
9. Ibid., pp. 456,457.
10. *Science and Health*, p. 139.
11. Ibid., p. 99.
12. Mary Baker Eddy, *Miscellaneous Writings*, 1883-1896 (Boston: First Church of Christ Scientist), p. 171.
13. *Science and Health*, p. 139.
14. Ibid., p. 334.
15. Ibid., p. 545.

For Further Reading

Hoekema, Anthony A., *The Four Major Cults*. Grand Rapids: Wm. B. Eerdmans Publishing Co., 1963.
Lewis, Gordon R., *Confronting the Cults*. Nutley, NJ: Presbyterian and Reformed Publishing Company, 1966.
Martin, Walter R., *The Kingdom of the Cults*. Grand Rapids: Zondervan Publishing House, 1961, 1965.
Robertson, Irvine., *What the Cults Believe*. Chicago: Moody Press, 1966.

12
Mormonism
A New "Prophet" Writes New "Scripture"

On the night of September 21, 1823, a praying boy of 17 looked up, and there was the angel Moroni standing by his bed. Moroni told the boy where he could find a set of golden plates—a book containing the "fulness of the everlasting Gospel" as delivered by the Saviour to the ancient inhabitants of America. This was the story as told by the boy, Joseph Smith, Jr.[1]

The next day, according to Smith, he found the plates buried in a stone box in the side of a hill called Cumorah near his home in Palmyra, New York. But Moroni would not let Smith have the plates until September 22, 1827.

Nine months before the plates became his, Smith eloped with Emma Hale. Smith said that, because of persecution, he moved to his wife's father's home in Harmony, Pennsylvania. It was there that he began to translate the plates with the aid of two magic stones, the "Urim" and the "Thummim."

A New York farmer named Martin Harris got interested

in Smith's project and planned to pay for publishing the book. But first, he wanted to make sure that it was genuine. Harris took Smith's copies of letters on the plates to Professor Charles Anthon of Columbia University. Smith later wrote that Anthon identified the letters as "Egyptian, Chaldaic, Assyriac, and Arabic," and said that Smith's translation was more accurate than "any he had before seen translated from the Egyptian."[2]

A professor's opinion of the "golden plates"

When Professor Anthon heard about Smith's claim, he wrote a letter dated February 17, 1834, to tell his side of the story:[3]

New York, N.Y., Feb. 17, 1834
Mr. E.D. Howe
Painesville, Ohio
Dear Sir:
   I received this morning your favor of the 9th instant and lose no time in making a reply. The whole story about my having pronounced the Mormonite inscription to be "reformed Egyptian hieroglyphics" is perfectly false. Some years ago, a plain and apparently simple-hearted farmer called upon me with a note from Dr. Mitchell of our city, now deceased, requesting me to decipher, if possible, a paper which the farmer would hand me, and which Dr. Mitchell confessed he had been unable to understand. Upon examining the paper in question, I soon came to the conclusion that it was all a trick, perhaps a hoax. When I asked the person who brought it how he obtained the writing, he gave me, as far I can now recollect, the following account: A "gold book," consisting of a number of plates of gold, fastened together in the shape of a book by wires of the same metal, had been dug up in the northern part of the state of New York, and along with the book an enormous pair of "gold spectacles." These

spectacles were so large, that if a person attempted to look through them, his two eyes would have to be turned towards one of the glasses merely, the spectacles being altogether too large for the breadth of the human face. Whoever examined the plates through the spectacles was enabled not only to read them, but fully to understand their meaning. All this knowledge however was confined at that time to a young man, who had the trunk containing the book and spectacles in his sole possession. This young man was placed behind a curtain, in the garret of a farm house, and being thus concealed from view, put on the spectacles occasionally, or rather looked through one of the glasses, deciphered the characters in the book, and having committed some of them to paper, handed copies from behind the curtain to those who stood on the outside. Not a word, however, was said about the plates having been deciphered "by the gift of God." Everything, in this way, was effected by the large pair of spectacles. The farmer added that he had been requested to contribute a sum of money towards the publication of the "golden book," the contents of which would, as he had been assured, produce an entire change in the world and save it from ruin. So urgent had been these solicitations, that he intended selling his farm and handing over the amount received to those who wished to publish the plates. As a last precautionary step, however, he had resolved to come to New York and obtain the opinion of the learned about the meaning of the paper which he had brought with him and which had been given him as a part of the contents of the book, although no translation had been furnished at the time by the young man with the spectacles. On hearing this odd story, I changed my opinion about the paper, and instead of viewing it any longer as a hoax upon the learned, I began to regard it as part of a scheme to cheat the farmer of his money and I communicated my suspicions to him, warning him to beware of rogues. He requested an opinion from me in writing, which of course I declined giving, and he took his leave carrying the paper with him. This paper was in fact a singular scrawl. It consisted of crooked characters disposed in columns and had evidently been prepared by some person who had before him at the time a book containing various alphabets. Greek and Hebrew letters, crosses and flourishes, Roman letters inverted or placed sideways, were arranged in perpendicular columns, and the whole ended in a rude delineation of a circle, divided into various compartments, decked with various strange marks, and evidently copied after the Mexican Calendar given by Humboldt, but copied in such a way as not to betray the source whence it was derived. I am thus particular as to the contents of the paper, inasmuch as I have frequently conversed with my friends on the subject, since the Mormonite excitement began, and well remember that the paper contained anything else but "Egyptian Hieroglyphics." . . .

I have thus given you a full statement of all that I know respecting the origin of Mormonism, and must beg you, as a personal favor, to publish this letter immediately should you find my name mentioned again by these wretched fanatics.

> *Yours respectfully,*
> *Charles Anthon, LL.D.*
> *Columbia University.*

The professor's warning had no effect on Martin Harris, for he mortgaged his farm to get money to publish, on March 26, 1830, the *Book of Mormon*. Harris later admitted that he never actually saw the plates since "they were covered over with a cloth."[4]

Two other men supposed to have seen the plates, Oliver Cowdery and David Whitmer, later left the Mormon church having been accused of theft and counterfeiting. Despite this, the *Testimony of Three Witnesses* (Harris, Cowdery and Whitmer) is found in the front of every copy of the *Book of Mormon*.

Is the Book of Mormon God's Word?

As stated in Article 8 of the Mormon Articles of Faith, they regard the *Book of Mormon* as the Word of God. Oddly enough, though supposedly translated from "reformed Egyptian" during the years between 1827 and 1830, the book is written in the same style as the King James Bible of 1611! By way of example, let's look at II Nephi 29:6,9,10:

"Thou fool, that shall say: A Bible, we have got a Bible, and we need no more Bible. . . . And because that I have spoken one word ye need not suppose that I cannot speak another. . . Wherefore, because that ye have a Bible ye need not suppose that it contains all my words; neither need ye suppose that I have not caused more to be written."

The *Book of Mormon* tells a remarkable story about two great migrations to North America.

The first migration took place about 2,250 B.C. when a group called Jaredites left the area of the Tower of Babel and crossed the Pacific in eight large boats. When they landed on the West Coast of Central America, they built large cities and prospered with the aid of many horses, asses, elephants, also "cureloms and cumoms." These latter are described as especially useful.[5]

But the Jaredites didn't get along very well with each other. After some terrific battles all but two, Coriantumr and Shiz, were killed. Coriantumr managed to cut off the head of Shiz so that "Shiz raised upon his hands and fell; and after that he had struggled for breath, he died" (Ether 15:31).

The second group to come to America, says the *Book of Mormon,* were Lehi and his family. Lehi was a Jewish Prophet who arrived about 600 B.C. He and his son Nephi built a boat and the whole family sailed to South America. But some families of Nephi and of his brother Laman rebelled against God who cursed them and made their skin black (II Nephi 5:21). Mormons believe that the American Indians are the descendants of Laman. This would make all Indians dark-skinned Israelites instead of Mongolians as all anthropologists claim.

The descendants of Nephi who did not rebel against God moved to Central and North America where they built a great civilization with large cities. In A.D. 34 Jesus Christ came to them from heaven, taught them about baptism and communion, and preached the entire Sermon on the Mount (III Nephi 11:28).

In A.D. 385 (near the hill Cumorah) all the Lamanites and Nephites were killed in a great battle. The only survivor was Moroni, the son of Mormon, who appeared to Joseph Smith, Jr.

Besides "translating" the *Book of Mormon,* Joseph Smith "revised" sections of the King James Bible. New revelations were added, especially in Genesis. These additions, quoted in *Pearl of Great Price,* state, for instance, that Satan wanted to redeem mankind but was refused by God, and that Adam was baptized by immersion.

Also added to Genesis 50 was a prophecy about the coming of Joseph Smith, Jr. himself: "And that seer I bless. . . and his name shall be called Joseph, and it shall be after the name of his father. . . for the thing which the Lord shall bring forth by his hand shall bring my people unto salvation."[6] Such scriptures are completely sacred to Mormons. A third book, *Doctrine and Covenants,* by Smith is also considered sacred.

How the Mormons migrated to Utah

By the time Joseph Smith was 25 years old (in 1830), he had organized a small group of followers into the "Church of Jesus Christ of Latter-day Saints." The next year, by "special revelation," he was told to leave the state of New York.

Smith led the nucleus of his church to Kirtland, Ohio, where the membership grew to 1,600. Then they all moved to "the land of Zion"—Zion, Missouri. Because they claimed the town "for the Lord"—that is, for themselves—they were driven out by the townspeople.

By 1839, they had moved to Illinois and were living in a community called Nauvoo (which Smith claimed was Hebrew for "beautiful place") on the Mississippi River. Soon the local newspaper, the *Nauvoo Expositor,* began to criticize the Mormons—for their belief in polygamy among other things. The Mormon "Legion" destroyed the newspaper office, and Smith was arrested. On June 27, 1844, an angry mob stormed the jail. Smith was shot and Mormonism had its first martyr.

Now Brigham Young assumed leadership and led the entire group on a long, dangerous journey across the plains. On July 24, 1847, they arrived at the great Salt Lake in Utah and Young announced, "This is the place!" It has been *the* place for Mormons ever since.

Membership of the Mormon church now exceeds 2.5 million in the United States alone. About seven out of every eight Mormons live in the United States, the majority in Utah. Their Mecca is temple headquarters in Salt Lake City, but there are important temples in Los Angeles, Hawaii, Switzerland and nine other places around the world. The temple is sacred to Mormons, for only there the ceremonies of celestial marriage and baptism for the dead are performed.

These practices have great saving power according to Mormon doctrine. Oddly enough, they do not appear in the *Book of Mormon,* but were added later by Smith in his *Doctrine and Covenants.*

From new revelation to "new doctrines"

Once Joseph Smith had his premise of new revelation established with the *Book of Mormon,* he then wrote the two books that are the source of most of the anti-Christian doctrines in Mormonism: *The Pearl of Great Price* and *Doctrine and Covenants.*

For example, Mormons have an unbiblical view of the doctrine of God. They claim that God is not a Spirit, but is of material substance. They also say that there are many gods (polytheism) and that men are gods.

In his *Journal of Discourses,* Joseph Smith wrote, "God himself was once as we are now and is an exalted man.[7] Smith also wrote in *Doctrine and Covenants,* "The father had a body of flesh and bone as tangible as man's."[8] And, in his sermon, "The Christian Godhead—Plurality of Gods," Joseph Smith declared, "The doctrine of a plurality of Gods is as prominent in the Bible as any other doctrine. It is all over the face of the Bible. It stands beyond the power of controversy. . . The heads of the gods appointed one God for us; and when you take that view of the subject, it sets one free to see the beauty, holiness and perfection of the Gods."[9]

The Bible states that there is but one God and declares that God is a Spirit (see John 4:24). Mormons cannot argue with such a point-blank statement, so Joseph Smith offered his own "inspired version" of that verse which completely alters the meaning of it. According to Smith the verse reads, "God has promised His Spirit" instead of "God is a Spirit." All Greek scholars, however, past and present, agree that the verse reads, "God is a Spirit." There is no other meaning—unless someone (such as Joseph Smith) arbitrarily decides to make Greek say what he wants it to say.

From this distorted view of God, Mormons go on to explain sin. The original sin was not such a bad thing in the eyes of Mormons. In fact, they teach that it was necessary for Adam and Eve to sin. Mormon Eldon Hicks, in his book *Combination Reference,* states: "The fall of Adam and Eve was a necessary change. . . in order to provide mortal parentage for the spirit children of God who were ready and waiting for the experience of earth life."[10] This teaching is in keeping with their view of the nature of man as divine—progressing toward godhood. By admitting this premise, it is no wonder that Mormons find no fault with polygamy (plural marriage).

When Joseph Smith founded the cult in the late 1820s, he included this warning in his *Book of Mormon*: "There shall not any man among you have save it be one wife; and concubines he shall have none."[11]

But a few years later, Smith was given "a special revelation" which allowed polygamy. Smith himself had nearly 50 wives. Brigham Young, Smith's successor, married 27 wives and fathered 56 children.

When the practice of polygamy prevented Utah's entrance into the Union in 1890, a Mormon official conveniently had a revelation that supposedly condemned polygamy. Actually, the Mormon doctrinal system encourages and condones polygamy. According to Mormon doctrine, celestial marriages are continually producing spirit children who are waiting to be born of mortal parents so they can then earn salvation into the Celestial Kingdom. It follows that a good Mormon will have as many wives and children as possible so these spirit children can be born. Many Mormons practice polygamy in secret even though their church officially disapproves. Despite Mormon denials, the practice of polygamy continues today in a sect which calls itself Fundamentalist Mormons.

According to an article in the June, 1967 *Ladies Home Journal*, there are 10,000 polygamous families living in metropolitan Salt Lake City alone. William Rogers, former special assistant to the Utah State Attorney General, states, "Today in Utah there are more polygamous families than in the days of Brigham Young. At least 30,000 men, women and children in this state are now living in plural households—and the number is rapidly increasing."[12]

"In 1965, for an article on Mormonism—the normally circumspect *New York Times* concluded. . . 'It is entirely possible that more people live in polygamy in Utah today than did between 1852 and 1890, a period when the Latter-day Saints Church openly advocated the practice.' ''[13]

Other views which relate to the Mormon doctrine of plural marriages are those of Jesus' birth and the wedding at Cana attended by the Lord. Mormons say that our Saviour was produced, not by a direct act of the Holy Spirit, but by actual sexual relations between a resurrected Adam-god and Mary. They further assert that the wedding Jesus attended in Cana where He turned water into wine was His own. Brigham Young wrote that Jesus married Lazarus's sisters, Mary and Martha, that day—and that He also married Mary Magdalene.

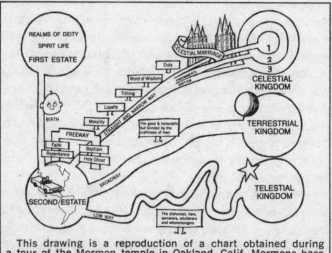

This drawing is a reproduction of a chart obtained during a tour of the Mormon temple in Oakland, Calif. Mormons base their three-storied view of heaven on the writings of Joseph Smith, who wrote: "In Mormon theology, there are three heavens: the telestial, the terrestrial and the celestial. The first heaven is designed for heathen people who rejected the Gospel . . . The second heaven will be inhabited by Christians who did not accept the Mormon message, along with men of good will of other religions who rejected the revelations of the saints. The final or celestial heaven is itself divided into three kingdoms, the highest of which is godhood or the possession of a kingdom for one's self and one's family . . ." (From **Doctrine** and **Covenants**, Section 130, verse 22.)

These views sound like the pagan ideas of ancient days, with deification of sex and fertility, in which the gods married mortals. These doctrines hardly need further commentary. With these perverted views of God, sin, man and marriage, it is not difficult to understand Joseph Smith's concept of salvation and heaven. He taught that heaven had three divisions— the Telestial, Terrestrial, and Celestial kingdoms. (See diagram 2.) All men, say Mormons, will be "saved" and included in one of these three levels of heaven.

Actually, Mormonism teaches salvation by faith *plus* works (as the church outlines them) *plus* baptism. Mormons teach that the dead can be baptized by proxy for salvation.

Mormons believe that the family unit will endure unto the eternal ages, that those in heaven, as gods, will produce spirit children. That is why they place so much emphasis on plural marriage and baptismal rites for the dead.

Celestial marriage is a ritual that must take place in a Mormon temple. When the couple is married according to this ritual, they are considered "sealed" in marriage for eternity. In other words, after they die and go to heaven, they will still be married and will be able to produce children.

This contradicts Jesus Christ who said, "At the resurrection people will neither marry nor be given in marriage; they will be like the angels in heaven" (Matt. 22:30).

Another necessary ritual is baptism for the dead. This is believed to give eternal life to those who have already died. A Mormon traces his family records to find as many ancestral names as he can. He then goes to a temple and is baptized by immersion for each of his ancestors. This gains both the Mormon and his dead relatives eternal life.

Mormons base their "baptism for the dead" doctrine on 1 Corinthians 15:29: "Now if there is no resurrection, what will these do who are baptized for the dead? If the dead are not raised at all, why are people baptized for them?"

While it is true that Bible scholars are divided on the

precise interpretation of this portion of Scripture it is obvious that the verse does not mean that someone could be literally baptized in place of a dead relative and in so doing obtain salvation for a relative who had made no act of personal commitment to Jesus Christ while he was living!

The clear teaching of Scripture is that man shall believe on the Lord Jesus Christ and be saved. Salvation is an individual matter that every person must settle with God during his life on earth. Scripture teaches that salvation is personal—not by proxy. (See Acts 16:31; Rom. 10:1,10; John 1:12.) The context from which 1 Corinthians 15:29 is taken shows that Paul is discussing Christians and their hope in the Resurrection. In the entire fifteenth chapter of 1 Corinthians, Paul is talking about people who have believed in Jesus Christ and who have known Him as their personal Saviour.

The entire Mormon system is based in the ''revealed'' writing of one man, Joseph Smith. The *Book of Mormon* has been proven incorrect by archaeologists, anthropologists, and Bible scholars.

Smith's other writings, *The Pearl of Great Price* and *Doctrine and Covenants,* are the seedbed of a theology that completely refutes and contradicts the historic, orthodox Christian faith.

Mormonism puts a good emphasis on clean living and good works, but the best that can be said for its theology was written by Walter Martin in *Kingdom of the Cults:* ''One can search the corridors of pagan mythology and never equal the complex structure which the Mormons have erected and masked under the terminology and misnomer of orthodox Christianity.''[14]

What's the difference?

Christians	*Mormons*
	GOD
God is uniquely eternal and	God is a material creature

all powerful, the only God— and He is a Spirit (Ps. 145:13; John 4:24; 1 Tim. 1:17).

who was once a man as we are now men. They say men can finally achieve godhood through works and that there are many gods.

THE BIBLE

The Bible, given by God's Spirit, is complete in itself and needs no additions. In fact, additions to the Bible are forbidden (Deut. 4:2; 12:32; Prov. 30:5,6; Gal. 1:8; Heb. 1:1,2; Rev. 22:18,19).

They have "new Scripture" and the writings of Joseph Smith are divinely inspired revelations—God's nineteenth century additions to the Bible.

SIN

Man is not godlike, but sinful and separated from God. Man can only approach God and have a relationship with Him through faith in Christ. Man, apart from Christ, is lost. (See Rom. 5:12-19; 6:23; Eph. 2:1,2; John 1:29; Gal. 3:13).

Man is progressively becoming a god. Mormons teach that Adam's sin in Eden was necessary in order to provide parentage for the spirit children of God who were ready and waiting for the experience of earth life.

SALVATION

Salvation is a free gift provided by the grace (unmerited love) of God for all who believe and accept His plan (Eph. 2:8,9; John 12:26; 14:1-3,6; 1 John 3:1,2).

Salvation comes by works and all men will spend eternity on some level of a multistoried heaven. The level will be determined by the scope each man's good works.

Notes

1. *Messenger and Advocate,* vol. 1, pp. 78,79. Quoted in Tanner, *The First Vision Examined* (Salt Lake City: Modern Microfilm Co., 1969), p. 15.

2. Joseph Smith, *Pearl of Great Price* (Salt Lake City: Church of Jesus Christ of Latter-day Saints), p. 52.

3. Letter from Professor Charles Anthon to E.O. Howe, February 17, 1834. Quoted by Tanner in *Mormonism: Shadow or Reality* (Salt Lake City: Modern Microfilm Co., 1972), p. 105.

4. Robert F. Boyd, "Mormonism," *Interpretation,* X, no. 4 (October 1951), p. 431.

5. Joseph Smith, *Book of Mormon* (Salt Lake City: Church of Jesus Christ of Latter-day Saints), Ether 9:19.

6. Joseph Smith, *Inspired Version of the Holy Scriptures* (Independence, MO: Herald Publishing House, 1955), Genesis 50:33.

7. *Journal of Discourses,* vol. 6, p. 3.

8. *Doctrine and Covenants,* 130:22.

9. Joseph Fielding Smith, *Teachings of the Prophet Joseph Smith* (Salt Lake City: Deseret Book Co., 1958), pp. 370, 372.

10. Eldon Hicks, *Combination Reference.*

11. *Book of Mormon,* Jacob 2:27.

12. Ben Meron, "More than One Wife," *Ladies Home Journal* (June, 1967).

13. Gary Jennings, "Polygamy," *Cosmopolitan* magazine (June, 1967).

14. Walter Martin, *Kingdom of the Cults* (Grand Rapids: Zondervan Publishing House, 1965), p. 181.

For Further Reading

Bjornstad, James. *Counterfeits at Your Door* (Glendale, CA: Regal Books, 1979).

Fraser, Gordon H. *Is Mormonism Christian?* Chicago: Moody Press, 1977.

Tanner, Jerald and Sandra. *The Changing World of Mormonism.* Chicago: Moody Press, 1979.

McElveen, Floyd. *The Mormon Illusion* (Glendale, CA: Regal Books, 1979).